Spectator's Guide to the 1980 Olympics

Grolier Enterprises Inc.
Danbury, Connecticut

Grolier Incorporated

PRESIDENT
and CHIEF EXECUTIVE OFFICER: Robert B. Clarke

SENIOR VICE PRESIDENT,
PUBLISHING: Howard B. Graham

VICE PRESIDENT
EDITORIAL DIRECTOR: Wallace S. Murray

Grolier Enterprises Inc.

PRESIDENT
and PUBLISHER: Robert W. Schramke

EXECUTIVE VICE PRESIDENT,
ASSOCIATE PUBLISHER: Dante Cirilli

SENIOR VICE PRESIDENT,
ASSOCIATE PUBLISHER: Henry J. Lefcort

TEXT BY: Jeffrey H. Hacker

DESIGN: Abbie Carroll Wilson

EDITORS: James E. Churchill, Jr.
Edward Humphrey

EDITORIAL ASSISTANT: Doris Lechner

DIRECTOR OF MANUFACTURING: Dale E. Bowman

MANAGER,
MAIL ORDER MANUFACTURING: David Bonjour

MANAGER,
PRE-PRESS SERVICES: Elizabeth Chase

ASSISTANT
PRE-PRESS SERVICES: Alan Phelps

ISBN 0-7172-8152-3

The Library of Congress Catalog Card Number: 79-66059

COPYRIGHT © 1979 BY GROLIER ENTERPRISES, INC.
DANBURY, CONNECTICUT

TABLE OF CONTENTS

INTRODUCTION

The Olympic Games represent the largest regularly scheduled gathering of nations and people. Every four years the designated host cities of the Winter and Summer Games attract amateur athletes, sport fans, casual tourists, media personnel, and official representatives from all around the globe. Pageantry, ceremony, and a tradition of athletic excellence have made the Olympics the most celebrated sporting event of our time.

But even as the Games have become more elaborate and widely attended, the most important reason for their ever-increasing popularity no doubt has been the increasing amount of television coverage. Since the first satellite transmission of the Olympic Games in 1960, more hours have been televised to more countries with each celebration. The pattern continues in 1980, as ABC's planned coverage of the Winter Games and NBC's coverage of the Summer Games will be more extensive and more technologically sophisticated than ever before.

And for good reasons. Restrictions on the number of tickets available to each country, the difficulties and expense of traveling to Lake Placid or Moscow, the lack of accommodations, to say nothing of the discomforts of standing in the cold amid the throng of spectators at the ski jumping competition or the exasperations of sitting in the last row of the gymnastics arena trying to distinguish Nadia Comaneci from Kurt Thomas, all add to the appeal of television viewing.

Television viewers can have the best seats in the house for each and every event. All in all, the best arrangements for the 1980 Olympics would be to set aside some time, make sure the TV is working, and claim rights to your favorite armchair for two weeks in February and three weeks during July and August.

For the casual spectator and ardent fan alike, full enjoyment of the Olympic Games rests upon a basic knowledge of the individual sports and a way of assessing the performances of the winning athletes. There are certain to be aspects of the Games that even veteran followers do not fully understand or appreciate. What is the biathlon? What are the rules of team handball? Not everyone will be in the embarrassing position of the U.S. Congressman who, not many years back, asked if the luge was "something to eat." The very helpful TV commentators surely will inform their audience that the luge is a small sled raced down a curved ice chute, but there will be many other insights and perspectives that TV time simply will not be extensive enough to cover.

Therefore, this book. In addition to the complete schedules of events for the Winter and Summer Games, television timetables, insights into the technological innovations of the 1980 telecasts, and a description of the facilities in Lake Placid and in Moscow, the *Spectator's Guide to the 1980 Olympics* provides detailed and general information on the rules and regulations, history, outstanding competitors, trends and developments, and some finer points of each sport on the program.

Such information is more than a summary of any official, all-inclusive text. The rules for the Olympic sports are not established by the International Olympic Committee (IOC), but by a designated governing body *for each sport.* (The name of each federation is given in the appropriate article. The acronym following each name may not correspond exactly to the order of the initials because it derives from the untranslated title of the organization.)

Because the various governing bodies frequently make rule changes in the months just prior to the Olympics, and because of difficulties in obtaining some of the rulebooks, minor inaccuracies may occur. Neither is the history of the Olympics contained in any one formal or official account. Sports historians frequently disagree on the spelling of winners' names, records, and other factual details—especially in the early Games. For this guide, matters of conflict have been settled by recourse to Erich Kamper's thoroughly researched *Encyclopedia of the Olympic Games* 1972).

For the enjoyment and convenience of the reader, scorecard/summaries are provided on which to record the winners in each sport and, where appropriate, to compare their performances with the prior Olympic record. Because most of the measurements in the Olympics (length of races, height of jumps, weight of apparatuses, and official specifications for the size of fields and courses) are given in the metric system, the conversion table below will give the reader a quick translation to more familiar terms. At the end of the Winter and Summer Games, the reader can count up the medalists from each country, or look them up in the newspaper, and record the final medal standings on pages 31 and 96.

So keep this guide on hand as you watch the competitions in each sport—and happy viewing!

METRIC CONVERSION TABLE

1 centimeter (cm)	=	.39 in		
10 cm	=	3.94 in		
100 cm	=	39.37 in	=	3' 3½"
1 meter (m)	=	3' 3½"	=	1.09 yds
10 m	=	32' 10"	=	10.94 yds
50 m	=	164' 0"	=	54.68 yds
100 m	=	328' 1"	=	109.36 yds
1 000 m	=	1,093.6 yds	=	.62 mi
1 kilometer (km)	=	.62 mi		
10 km	=	6.21 mi		
50 km	=	31.0 mi		
100 km	=	62.1 mi		
1 gram (g)	=	.035 oz		
10 g	=	.35 oz		
100 g	=	3.53 oz		
1.000 g	=	35.27 oz	=	2 lbs 3 oz
1 kilogram (kg)	=	2 lbs 3 oz		
5 kg	=	11 lbs		
10 kg	=	22 lbs 1 oz		
100 kg	=	220 lbs 7 oz		

SITES, SCHEDULES,
and
TELEVISION COVERAGE

On October 23, 1974, the International Olympic Committee (IOC) named Lake Placid, N.Y., as the site of the XIII Olympic Winter Games, February 12–24, 1980, and Moscow, USSR, as the host of the XXII Olympic Games, July 19–August 3, 1980. Exclusive television rights for the United States later were granted to the American Broadcasting Company (ABC) for the Winter Games and to the National Broadcasting Company (NBC) for the Summer Games.

LAKE PLACID

Lake Placid is a remote village deep in the Adirondack Mountains of northeastern New York State. The tiny winter resort has a year-round population of only 3,000 and is several hours' drive from the nearest city. Yet in many ways it is an ideal location for the 1980 Winter Olympics. The town was host to the very successful 1932 Games, and many of the facilities can be used again. The projected cost of the 1980 celebration, $150 million including administrative costs, is inexpensive compared, for example, to the $750 million spent on the 1972 Winter Games at Sapporo, Japan. Organizers and promoters describe it as a "no frills" operation which will "return the Games to the athletes." The inaccessibility of Lake Placid and the announced limit of 51,000 spectators per day (for environmental reasons) add special importance to the television coverage.

The Whiteface Mountain ski area, approximately 10 mi (16 km) from town, is the site of the downhill, slalom, and giant slalom events (*see* SKIING—Alpine). A special feature is a snowmaking system which will cover more than half of the 16 mi (26 km) of trails with man-made snow. Meanwhile, ABC is lacing the mountain with more than 33 mi (53 km) of camera and microphone cable, much of it buried. Approximately 18 television cameras will provide coverage of the competition from more than 60 different positions. The cameras will be relocated from slope to slope by helicopter.

The bobsled and luge runs (*see* BOBSLEDDING; LUGE) are on Mt. Van Hoevenberg, about 6½ mi (10½ km) from Lake Placid. The 1-mi (1.6-km) bobsled run was built for the 1932 Games and refurbished for the 1980 competition. The adjacent luge run is 1,000 m (1,094 yds) long and was built especially for 1980. Fourteen television cameras will cover the action from the two runs. Both areas are pre-cabled and the cameras will be transported between sites by special sleds.

The cross-country skiing and biathlon competitions are also being held on Mt. Van Hoevenberg. Over the years, the area has gained the reputation of having some of the world's best cross-country runs. The long trails through the woods make the laying of cables an impossible task. Self-contained, portable cameras likely will be used.

Intervale Hill on the edge of Lake Placid is the site of the ski jumping events. The jump used in the 1932 Games was demolished to make room

COMPETITION SCHEDULE
XIII OLYMPIC WINTER GAMES, FEBRUARY 1980

	OPENING CEREMONY	BIATHLON	BOBSLEDDING	FIGURE SKATING	ICE DANCING	ICE HOCKEY	LUGE	SKIING—Alpine	SKIING—Cross-Country	SKI JUMPING	SPEED SKATING	CLOSING CEREMONY
12 Tuesday						●						
13 Wednesday	●						●					
14 Thursday						●	●	●	●		●	
15 Friday			●	●	●		●		●		●	
16 Saturday		●	●			●	●				●	
17 Sunday				●	●			●	●	●	●	
18 Monday				●		●		●	●	●		
19 Tuesday		●		●	●		●	●	●		●	
20 Wednesday				●		●		●	●		●	
21 Thursday				●				●	●		●	
22 Friday		●				●		●				
23 Saturday			●	●				●	●	●	●	●
24 Sunday			●			●						

ABC's Telecast Schedule for the
1980 Olympic Winter Games
(Eastern Standard Time)

Tuesday, February 12	9:00–11:00 P.M.
Wednesday, February 13	2:00– 4:00 P.M. (Opening Ceremony) 9:00–11:00 P.M.
Thursday, February 14	8:30–11:00 P.M. 11:30–11:45 P.M.
Friday, February 15	8:30–11:00 P.M. 11:30–11:45 P.M.
Saturday, February 16	1:00– 3:30 P.M. 9:00–11:00 P.M. 11:30–11:45 P.M.
Sunday, February 17	1:00– 3:30 P.M. 8:00–11:00 P.M. 11:30–11:45 P.M.
Monday, February 18	9:00–11:00 P.M. 11:30–11:45 P.M.
Tuesday, February 19	8:00–11:00 P.M. 11:30–11:45 P.M.
Wednesday, February 20	9:00–11:00 P.M. 11:30–11:45 P.M.
Thursday, February 21	8:00–11:00 P.M. 11:30–11:45 P.M.
Friday, February 22	9:00–11:00 P.M. 11:30–11:45 P.M.
Saturday, February 23	12:30– 3:30 P.M. 8:00–11:00 P.M. 11:30–11:45 P.M.
Sunday, February 24	12:00– 6:00 P.M. 8:00–11:00 P.M. (Closing Ceremony)

for new 70-m and 90-m hills. The two concrete towers stand side by side, and their long runways send the jumpers almost to the bottom of the landing area. Intervale presents no special logistical problems for telecasting, but, as at several other sites, excessive cold is a potential problem. Portable power generators may be required to keep the cameras warm.

The speed skating oval is located in the center of town on the grounds of Lake Placid High School. The oval was used in 1932, but a new refrigeration system has been installed. The cost of refurbishing the rink was approximately $3 million. There is only one other 400-m speed skating oval in the United States, in West Allis, Wis.

The new Olympic fieldhouse, site of the figure skating and ice hockey competition, contains two ice sheets and holds about 8,000 spectators. It connects with the Olympic Arena, which was built for the 1932 Olympics and refurbished for the XIII Winter Games in 1980. ABC will lay thousands of feet of cable and set up five separate mobile production units at the complex.

The most controversial new facility for the Lake Placid Games is the Olympic Village, located about 7 mi (11.3 km) west of town in the hamlet of Ray Brook. Eleven permanent buildings, spread out over 36 acres (14.6 h), were designed to house 1,200 athletes and 600 coaches, trainers, and officials. However, several teams made other living arrangements because of the small size of the rooms and the "penitentiary atmosphere" of the complex. The $49-million facility, which will be used as a minimum security prison after the Olympics, is surrounded by two 12-ft-high (3.7-m) electrically-charged wire fences. According to the original plans, two athletes would be quartered in a room 10' × 10' (3 m × 3 m)—the same size room that later would house a single prisoner. Subsequently, Lake Placid organizers decided to make four-person rooms into triples, triples into doubles, and doubles into singles. Additional lodgings were created by setting up house trailers within the secured area.

From the first ice hockey match on Tuesday, February 12 to the closing ceremonies on Sunday, February 24, ABC will provide an unprecedented 50½ hours of television coverage. This is 7 hours more than the coverage of the 1976 Games from Innsbruck. Much of the competition will be telecast live, and the schedule provides for daytime, weekend, prime time, and late night viewing. Late night programming includes special features and a wrap-up of the day's events.

With the dual responsibility of providing coverage for the rest of the world as well as the United States, ABC will have about 300% more equipment at Lake Placid than it had at Innsbruck. There will be nearly 100 conventional TV cameras, 9 portable mini-cameras, three dozen video tape machines, and 15 mobile units.

ABC Sports will have about 800 production supervisors, technical engineers, and support personnel, as well as a team of announcers familiar to past Olympics viewers, at Lake Placid. Jim McKay will be the anchorman, with color commentary and backup coverage by Frank Gifford and Keith Jackson. Expert commentators for the various sports include Bob Beattie, former coach of the U.S. Ski Team, for Alpine skiing; Dick Button, two-time Olympic gold medalist, for figure skating; and Art Devlin, a veteran U.S. Olympian, for ski jumping.

MOSCOW

Moscow, the capital and largest city of the Soviet Union, has undergone enormous change in the 60 years since the October Revolution. Highways, housing developments, a subway system, factories, theaters, concert halls, and other additions have made it an important industrial, economic, and cultural center. And by the opening of the XXII Olympic Games on July 19, 1980, the 7.7 million residents of Moscow will have witnessed another major face-lift of their city. Eleven new sports centers will have been built, and an equal number will have been renovated or expanded. In addition, there will be a spacious new Olympic Village, a television broadcast center, press headquarters, 35-story hotel, international post office, computer center, and other structures that fit into a general development plan for the city. Government officials maintain that nothing is being built solely for the Olympics, and the cost of putting on the Games is therefore difficult to estimate. The head of the Olympic Organizing Committee put the figure at about $330 to $345 million.

The 1980 Games mark the first time that the Olympics are being held in a socialist country. As in the past, the celebration will be a showcase for the host city. Soviet organizers have predicted that the XXII Olympic Games will be the greatest ever, a major event in human history. The preparations have been lavish, and every attempt has been made to comply with Olympic rules and to make all visitors as comfortable as possible. U.S. tourists were promised a taste of home with the designation of Coca-Cola ("Koka Kora") as the official soft drink of the 1980 Olympics. Still, this first major exposure of the socialist bloc to Western culture has caused some worry among government leaders. Viktor Grishin, the head of the Moscow party committee and a member of the nation's ruling Politburo, expressed his concern in a speech given more than a year before the opening of the Games. Said Grishin: "It is necessary to insure that, in relations with foreigners, residents of the capital show cordiality and hospitality, stress the advantages of the Soviet way of life and the achievements of our society, and at the same time repulse the propaganda of alien ideas and principles, and the onslaughts on our country and on the ideas of communism and socialism."

The hub of the 1980 Olympic Games is the Central Lenin Stadium sports complex in the Luzhniki section of Moscow. The main stadium, which seats approximately 103,000, is the site of the opening and closing ceremonies, track and field events, soccer finals, and equestrian team jumping competitions. The Palace of Sports is a multipurpose indoor stadium adjacent to the main Stadium. The 10,000-seat arena is the site of the gymnastics and judo competitions. The Lenin sports complex also includes the Small Arena, with a capacity of 9,100 spectators, where the volleyball matches will be held, and a swimming pool for the water polo tournament. The entire complex has undergone extensive renovation in the three years preceding the Games.

Perhaps the most impressive new facility is a domed arena on Prospekt Mira, about 6 mi (10 km) from Lenin Stadium near the center of Moscow. With a seating capacity of 45,000, it is the largest indoor stadium in Europe. An enormous sliding door divides the arena in half, allowing the basketball and boxing matches to be held simultaneously. The swimming and diving events also will be held on Prospekt Mira, in a new aquatic center that seats about 15,000.

Another major construction project for the Soviets was a new sports complex at Krylatskoye, a suburb about 6 mi west of the city. The com-

COMPETITION SCHEDULE*

	OPENING CEREMONY	ARCHERY	BASKETBALL	BOXING	CANOEING & KAYAKING	CYCLING	EQUESTRIAN	FENCING	FIELD HOCKEY	GYMNASTICS
JULY 19 Saturday	●									
20 Sunday			●	●		●			●	●
21 Monday			●	●					●	●
22 Tuesday			●	●		●		●	●	●
23 Wednesday			●	●		●		●		●
24 Thursday			●	●		●	●	●	●	●
25 Friday			●	●		●	●	●	●	●
26 Saturday			●	●		●	●	●	●	
27 Sunday			●	●			●	●	●	
28 Monday			●	●		●		●	●	
29 Tuesday			●	●			●	●	●	
30 Wednesday		●	●	●	●		●	●	●	
31 Thursday		●		●	●		●	●	●	
AUGUST 1 Friday		●			●		●		●	
2 Saturday		●			●	●				
3 Sunday							●			

*As approved by the 79th Session of the IOC on June 16, 1977

XXII OLYMPIC GAMES, 1980

HANDBALL	JUDO	MODERN PENTATHLON	ROWING	SHOOTING	SOCCER	SWIMMING & DIVING	TRACK & FIELD	VOLLEYBALL	WATER POLO	WEIGHTLIFTING	WRESTLING—Freestyle	WRESTLING—Greco-Roman	YACHTING	CLOSING CEREMONY
●		●	●	●	●	●		●		●		●		
●		●	●	●	●	●		●		●		●	●	
●		●	●	●	●	●		●		●		●	●	
●		●	●	●	●	●		●	●	●		●	●	
●		●	●	●	●	●	●	●	●	●			●	
●			●	●	●	●	●	●	●					
●			●	●		●	●	●		●				
●	●		●		●	●	●	●	●	●	●		●	
●	●					●	●	●	●	●	●		●	
●	●				●	●		●	●	●	●		●	
●	●						●	●		●	●			
	●						●	●	●			●		
	●				●		●	●	●					
	●			●				●						
														●

plex includes one of the world's best rowing canals, archery fields, and a cycling track. Weightlifting competition will be held at a new facility in Izmailovo, on the northeast fringe of Moscow; shooting at a new range in the northern suburb of Mytishchi; the equestrian events at a new riding installation in Bitsa forest; men's team handball at Sokolniki Sports Palace between Prospekt Mira and Izmailovo; fencing and wrestling, at the Central Army Sports Club; and women's handball, field hockey, and part of the soccer tournament at the nearby Dynamo Sports Complex.

The only events not being held in or near Moscow are yachting and most of the soccer matches. The yacht races will take place in the Baltic Sea near Tallinn, Estonia, about 550 mi (885 km) west of Moscow. The elimination matches of the soccer tournament are being played at Kirov Stadium in Leningrad, Central Republican Stadium in Kiev, Dynamo Stadium in Minsk, and, as mentioned above, at Moscow's Dynamo Stadium. These facilities have been either modernized or totally reconstructed for the competition.

The athletes will be housed at the massive Olympic Village, which covers some 264 acres (107 h) in southwest Moscow. The village includes eighteen 16-story apartment houses, administrative buildings, a department store, restaurants, concert and dance halls, and elaborate training facilities. After the Olympics, the village will be used for city housing.

One of the facilities most vital to the XXII Olympic Games is the television and radio complex in the Ostankino section of Moscow. The existing broadcast center is the largest in Europe and boasts the world's highest ferro-concrete TV tower. A new 5-story superstructure, called OTBC-80, contains 72 radio booths, 22 television studios, and the latest electronic equipment. The installation will enable an estimated **2.5 billion** people around the world to watch the Moscow Games on television. The Games will be broadcast on 100 radio channels and 18 to 20 color and black-and-white television channels. The telecasts will be made possible by two satellites, one launched just before the start of the Games.

NBC, which has its own production center, paid a reported $85 million for the exclusive right to televise the 1980 Olympics in the United States. Chester R. Simmons, the former president of NBC Sports, expects the XXII Games to be the "biggest event in television history." The 16 days of coverage will be carried by 211 NBC affiliate stations. More than 170 million Americans are expected to watch.

NBC will provide 152 hours of programming, almost double the number of 1976. The tentative schedule calls for 67.5 hours of evening (8–11 p.m.) viewing; 25.5 hours of weekend viewing; 13 hours of late night time; and 46 hours in the daytime, early morning, and on Saturday morning. (Consult local listings for the exact timetable.) The network hopes to televise competition in *all* the sports, much of it live. It will employ more than 250 cameras, including 45 mini-cameras, and about 60 portable videotape machines.

The anchorman for most of the prime time telecasts will be veteran sports announcer Dick Enberg. Enberg will be assisted in the general coverage by Curt Gowdy and Jim Simpson, among others. NBC has also assembled an impressive team of specialists to describe and analyze the competition in each sport. Among them are former Olympians Bruce Jenner for track and field, John Naber and Donna de Verona for swimming, and Micki King Hogue for diving.

THE
WINTER
PROGRAM

February 12–February 24, 1980
Lake Placid, N.Y.

According to the Olympic Charter, the only sports that may be included in the men's program of the Winter Games are those that are widely practiced in 25 countries and on two continents; sports for women must be widely practiced in 20 countries and on two continents. The program may include skiing, skating, ice hockey, bobsledding, biathlon, and luge.

The schedule for the XIII Olympic Winter Games at Lake Placid, N.Y., includes 38 separate events in these six categories. The major difference from the 1976 program is the addition of one new event: the 10-km individual biathlon. Six gold medals are being awarded in Alpine skiing, ten in Nordic skiing and ski jumping, nine in speed skating, three in figure skating, one in ice dancing, three in biathlon, three in luge, two in bobsledding, and one in ice hockey.

Approximately 1,400 athletes from some 35 nations will gather at Lake Placid for the 13-day event. Opening ceremonies are scheduled for Wednesday, February 13, but the lengthy ice hockey tournament begins the day before. Medals for hockey and figure skating are presented at the Olympic Center following the last competition in each event. Award ceremonies for all other events are held each evening at 7:30, from February 14 through February 23, at Mirror Lake. The closing ceremony is scheduled for Sunday, February 24 at 9:30 P.M., at the athletic center.

A special arts festival at several locations in the Adirondack Mountains will coincide with the athletic competition. The program includes world premiere performances in classical music, jazz, and theater, as well as exhibitions of sculpture, paintings, photography, and other art forms.

THE OLYMPIC WINTER GAMES

YEAR	SITE	NUMBER OF NATIONS REPRESENTED	NUMBER OF ATHLETES PARTICIPATING
1924	Chamonix, France	16	293
1928	St. Moritz, Switzerland	25	491
1932	Lake Placid, N.Y., USA	17	307
1936	Garmisch-Partenkirchen, Germany	28	756
1948	St. Moritz, Switzerland	28	713
1952	Oslo, Norway	30	732
1956	Cortina d'Ampezzo, Italy	32	924
1960	Squaw Valley, Calif., USA	30	693
1964	Innsbruck, Austria	36	1,332
1968	Grenoble, France	37	1,272
1972	Sapporo, Japan	35	1,125
1976	Innsbruck, Austria,	37	1,054
1980	Lake Placid, N.Y., USA	35 (est.)	1,400 (est.)

BIATHLON

Dates: February 16, 19, 22
Location: Mt. Van Hoevenberg, N.Y.
Number of Events: 3
Held for: men only

The biathlon is one of the least known and most grueling events in the Winter Olympics. It requires a high degree of skill in two unrelated and dissimilar sports—cross-country skiing and rifle shooting. The participant must ski to four different shooting ranges along a course of varied terrain. He then fires a rifle at a target 100 to 250 m (328—820 ft) away. The most important ingredient of success is mental discipline—the ability to race swiftly over the rugged cross-country course and then shoot a rifle with the calm steady accuracy of a marksman.

Each biathlete is given a map of the course at least 48 hours before the competition. Practice runs are forbidden. The type of ski is optional, but automatic rifles and telescopic sights are not allowed. The skier must carry his rifle and ammunition with him. One competitor begins the course every two minutes and upon reaching each firing range is assigned a target. He loads the rifle and fires several rounds from a standing, kneeling, or prone position. The winner is determined on the basis of least time spent on the course, and penalty minutes are tacked on for each miss of the target. The official governing body for the Olympic biathlon competition is the International Modern Pentathlon and Biathlon Union (UIPMB). The rules for the skiing part of the event are those of the International Skiing Federation (FIS), while the rules for the shooting portion are those established by the International Shooting Union (UIT).

The Lake Placid Games of 1980 include the 20-km individual biathlon on February 16; the 10-km individual biathlon on Febuary 19; and the 4 × 7.5-km team relay on February 22. The 10-km event is being held for the first time.

Unnatural as it may seem, the combination of skiing and shooting is a familiar one in countries where military ski training is conducted. It is not surprising, therefore, that many biathlon champions are, or once were, in the service of their country. It is also not surprising that every medal awarded since the first Olympic biathlon competition in 1960 has gone to one of the Scandinavian countries, the Soviet Union, or East Germany. The Soviet Union has won every team event beginning with the first in 1968.

1980 SUMMARY

EVENT	GOLD MEDAL WINNER	COUNTRY
10-km Individual:		
20-km Individual:		
30-km Relay:		

BOBSLEDDING

Dates: February 15–16, 23–24
Location: Mt. Van Hoevenberg, N.Y.
Number of Events: 2
Held for: men only

Bobsled racing has aptly been referred to as "the champagne of thrills." Few sports are as exciting or as dangerous as careening down a mile-long, curved ice chute in a streamlined metal shell at a speed of almost 90 miles (145 km) per hour.

The Olympic bobsled run near Lake Placid was constructed for the 1932 Winter Games. Its original length was 1.5 mi (2.4 km), but it was later shortened to the present 1 mi (1.6 km). Refrigeration pipes, lighting, and a new underpass were added for 1980. The XIII Winter Games include two bobsledding events: two-man and four-man. In each event there is a total of four heats. Medal winners are determined on the basis of total time for all four heats. In the two-man competition, heats 1 and 2 are to be held on Friday, February 15; heats 3 and 4 the next day. In the four-man event, heats 1 and 2 are to be held on Saturday, February 23; heats 3 and 4 on Sunday the 24th.

Four-man bobsledding was included in the first Olympic Winter Games in 1924. Switzerland came in first, Great Britain second, and Belgium third. The 1932 Games at Lake Placid were important for several reasons: the two-man event was introduced, metal runners were used for the first time, and the practice of sitting in the sled was made mandatory. The United States won both gold medals. Between 1932 and 1956, U.S. bobsledders won a total of 4 gold, 3 silver, and 5 bronze medals. They have not won any medals since that time. West Germany was outstanding in the 1972 Games, and East Germany came away with both gold medals in 1976.

An important factor in the success of a bobsled team is the combined weight of the vehicle and crew members. Accordingly, the International Bobsleigh and Tobogganing Federation (FIBT) has set firm weight standards. The bobsled itself has undergone few technical changes over the years. The sleds used in world-class competition today were designed about 15 years ago and can be bought in only one place—Cortina d'Ampezzo, Italy (site of the 1956 Winter Olympics). Meanwhile, U.S. engineers at the American Bobsled Research Association and elsewhere have been attempting to make basic design changes to create a faster vehicle. Whether their innovations can help the United States regain its Olympic supremacy is a question that can be answered only at Mt. Van Hoevenberg.

1980 SUMMARY		
EVENT	**GOLD MEDAL WINNERS**	**COUNTRY**
Two-man:		
Four-man:		

FIGURE SKATING

Dates: February 15, 17–21, 23
Location: Olympic Center, Lake Placid, N.Y.
Number of Events: 3
Held for: men, women, pairs

Mention of Olympic figure skating automatically brings to mind Sonja Henie, Dick Button, Peggy Fleming, or Dorothy Hamill performing triple Axel jumps, flying Camel spins, and double loops to the strains of Tchaikovsky or Richard Strauss. But Olympic figure skating requires more than the acrobatic flair displayed in free skating. The skaters are also tested for balance, footwork, overall coordination, and basic skills.

THE EVENTS

SAMPLE COMPULSORY FIGURE
PARAGRAPH DOUBLE THREE

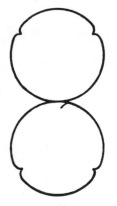

RfoTbiTfoiTboTfi—
LfiTboTfioTbiTfo

R = right foot
L = left foot
f = forward
b = backward
o = outside edge
i = inside edge
T = three (bracket)

Three figure skating competitions are held in the Olympic Games—men's singles, women's singles, and pairs. Single skating consists of "compulsory figures," a "short program" of required elements, and "free skating." Pairs skating (one woman and one man) consists of a short program and free skating.

The **compulsory** or "school" figures are two or three tangent circles, with instructions to the skater as to which edge of the blade and which foot to use in tracing them (see accompanying diagram). Each figure must be repeated three times consecutively. Each skater performs three figures. The accuracy of the tracings, cleanness of the lines, and graceful carriage of the skater are important considerations in scoring.

The **short program** in singles competition consists of seven required elements and connecting steps. The group of required elements that the International Skating Union (ISU) has designated for Olympic and championship competition in 1980 consists of the following jumps, spins, and steps: double toe Salchow; double Axel Paulsen (one and one-half revolutions each); combination of two jumps, including a double loop; flying jump Camel spin, landing in sitting position; Camel spin with one foot change; spin combination with one foot change and two position changes; and a straight line step sequence. The short program for pairs skating consists of six elements and connecting steps. The group selected for 1980 comprises the following: double flip (solo jump); overhead one-arm Axel lift; death spiral backward inside; change sit spin (solo spin); catch-waist Camel spin; and a serpentine step sequence.

Free skating is the most exciting and colorful part of the competition. The program must be a well balanced sequence of the skater's chosen movements performed to music. The maximum length of the program is 5 minutes for men's singles and pairs, 3 minutes for women's singles.

SCORING

All aspects of the figure skating competition are scored on a scale of 0 to 6. The score of 6 is awarded only for a figure or element that is "perfect and flawless." Each judge awards one mark for every compulsory figure. Two scores are given in the short program—execution of required elements and overall presentation. Two marks are also given in free skating—technical merit and artistic expression.

In the singles events, the marks for the three compulsory figures are added up and the sum is divided by 2.5; the two marks for the short program are also added together and divided by 2.5. These totals are added to the two marks for free skating to give the final score for each judge. In pairs competition, the marks for the short program are added together and the sum is divided by 2.5. The total points for free skating are then added to the points for the short program to give the final sum for each judge. The individual or pair placed first by the majority of judges is declared the winner.

1980 SUMMARY

EVENT	GOLD MEDAL WINNER	COUNTRY
Men's Singles:		
Women's Singles:		
Pairs:		

ICE DANCING

Dates: February 15, 17, 19
Location: Olympic Center, Lake Placid, N.Y.
Number of Events: 1
Held for: men and women (pairs)

Ice dancing is the newest sport in the Olympic Winter Games, having been held for the first time in 1976. It is closely related to pairs figure skating but differs in a fundamental way. In ice dancing there is greater emphasis on controlled movement and the continuous, rhythmic flow of formal dance steps. The woman's steps are usually more difficult than the man's, but it is important that the skaters stay close together.

The Olympic ice dancing competition consists of two parts: compulsory and free dancing. Both are performed to music. Among the dances listed by the International Skating Union (ISU) are the European waltz, fox-trot, fourteen-step, tango, rumba, and paso doble. Unlike compulsory dancing, the free dance does not have a specified sequence of steps. It is a series of original movements organized into a routine approximately 4 minutes long. The competitors are given scores (from 0 to 6) on the basis of skill and originality. The pair with the highest combined score for compulsory and free dancing is declared the winner.

1980 SUMMARY

EVENT	GOLD MEDAL WINNER	COUNTRY
Ice Dancing:		

ICE HOCKEY

Dates: February 12, 14, 16, 18, 20, 22, 24
Location: Olympic Center, Lake Placid, N.Y.
Number of Events: 1 tournament
Held for: men only

Ice hockey is the world's fastest team sport and the only one played at the Olympic Winter Games. Although most U.S. and Canadian stars play *professionally* in the National Hockey League (NHL), the Olympic tournament is the most important competition for *amateur* players throughout the world.

FORMAT

Twelve teams are participating in the 35-game tournament at Lake Placid's Olympic Center. Eight teams qualified on the basis of their participation in the 1979 World Championships. Those eight teams are: the Soviet Union, United States, Canada, Czechoslovakia, Sweden, West Germany, Finland, and Poland. The four others are Rumania, Japan, Norway, and The Netherlands. The 12 teams are divided into two groups of 6; they play a round-robin schedule within each group. The top two teams in each group proceed to the semifinal round. This is held on a "crossover" basis, with the first-place finisher in each group playing the second-place finisher in the other group. The two winners in the semifinal round play each other for the gold and silver medals; the two losing teams in the semifinal round play each other for third and fourth place.

THE GAME OF HOCKEY

The Olympic arena at Lake Placid contains two ice sheets—one is the standard U.S. size of 85 ft × 200 ft, the other the Olympic size of 30 m × 60 m. A hockey rink (*see diagram*) is divided by colored lines into three equal zones (offensive, neutral, and defensive), with a goal at each end. The object is to shoot a hard rubber puck into the opponent's

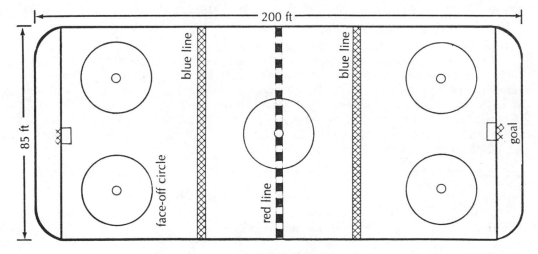

OLYMPIC ICE HOCKEY RINK

goal with a wooden stick. Each team consists of a goalie, two defense-men, a center, and two forwards. Because of the speed of the game, all players except the goalie are substituted for as often as every 2–3 minutes.

EQUIPMENT

Ice hockey skates differ significantly from figure skates: the boot has a lower ankle support; the blade is straight, narrow, and pointed in the front; and the stanchions (upright pieces of metal joining the sole of the boot with the blade) are higher. Hockey sticks are made of ash and rock-elm; the goalie's stick is heavier and wider than those of the other players. The puck itself is made of vulcanized rubber and is 1 inch (2.54 cm) thick and 3 inches (7.62 cm) in circumference. Other equipment includes shin guards, heavy gloves, a mouthpiece, and a helmet. The goalie wears extra padding and a special face mask.

HISTORY

The modern game of ice hockey is said to have been born on March 3, 1875, at the Victoria Skating Rink in Montreal, Canada. John Creighton, an engineer and amateur rugby player, is credited with laying down the first rules. The sport made its Olympic debut at the 1920 Summer Games in Antwerp, Belgium. The team representing Canada won easily. The excitement of the tournament guaranteed a place for ice hockey in the first Winter Games in 1924. As the list of champions (below) indicates the Canadians dominated competition until 1956, when the Soviet Union took part for the first time. Except for a surprise victory by the host U.S. team in 1960, the Soviets have won every gold medal since 1956.

PAST CHAMPIONS

1920	Canada	1952	Canada
1924	Canada	1956	Soviet Union
1928	Canada	1960	United States
1932	Canada	1964	Soviet Union
1936	Great Britain	1968	Soviet Union
1948	Canada	1972	Soviet Union
	1976	Soviet Union	

1980 SUMMARY

CHAMPIONSHIP GAME

TEAMS   FINAL SCORE

FINAL STANDINGS

GOLD:

SILVER:

BRONZE:

LUGE

Dates: February 13–16, 19
Location: Mt. Van Hoevenberg
Number of Events: 3
Held for: men, women

OLYMPIC LUGE RUN
IN 1980

The diagram above outlines the newly constructed luge run at Mt. Van Hoevenberg, N.Y. Men's events begin at the top of the 1,000-m course, women's competition at the 740-m point. A highlight of the run is the dangerous Omega turn, visible at the center.

Luge (pronounced *loozh*) racing, which was added to the Winter Olympic program in 1964 is a sport similar to bobsledding. Competitors slide down an icy chute on flat sleds 40 cm (16 inches) wide and 100 cm (39 inches) long. Unlike bobsledders, who sit in heavy iron vehicles and have good control over speed and direction, lugers lie on their backs and maintain their balance only by holding on to a thin strap. They wear tight rubber suits to take full advantage of aerodynamics and consistently reach speeds of more than 50 miles (80 km) per hour. The sleds are made of cloth or canvas, weigh a maximum of 22 kg (48.4 lbs) for a one-man sled and 24 kg (52.8 lbs) for a two-man sled, and have no braking or mechanical steering devices.

At the 1980 Games in Lake Placid the standard luge events are being held: men's singles, women's singles, and men's two-seater. Each nation is allowed three entries in the men's singles competition, three in women's singles, and two in men's doubles. In men's and women's singles each luger has four runs, and final rankings are based on total time. The two-seater competition is run in two heats, with composite time again determining the winner.

According to the rules of the International Luge Federation (FIL), the official governing body for the Olympics, a luge run must be between 1,000 and 1,200 m (1,094 and 1,312 yds) long and between 1.35 and 1.5 m (4'5" and 4'11") wide. It must have one hairpin turn, one right turn, one "S", and one "labyrinth" (a series of quick turns). The descent must be between 9% and 12%.

The luge run at Lake Placid was constructed especially for the 1980 Olympics at a cost of some $4.8 million. The 1,000-m run is the first in the Western Hemisphere suitable for international competition. It is already widely regarded as one of the world's best. The facility was unveiled in February 1979 at a special pre-Olympic meet. East Germany, which has won 12 of the 36 Olympic medals ever awarded in luge competition, was the easy winner.

1980 SUMMARY

EVENT	GOLD MEDAL WINNER	COUNTRY
Men's Singles:		
Men's Two-Seater:		
Women's Singles:		

SKIING—Alpine

Dates: February 14, 17–23
Location: Whiteface Mountain, N.Y.
Number of Events: 6
Held for: men, women

"There is no other sensation quite like skiing," said Jean-Claude Killy, the phenomenal French Olympian who won all three Alpine events—slalom, giant slalom, and downhill—at the 1968 Winter Games in Grenoble, France. "It is a rare wine, a beautiful woman . . . unforgettable."

Whether it is the unique feeling described by Killy, the lure of a highly cherished Olympic medal, or the opportunity to ski on courses that officials describe as among the fastest and most challenging in the world, Alpine ski racing is attracting athletes from more countries than any other event at the 1980 Winter Games. The program again includes the downhill, slalom, and giant slalom for both men and women.

THE EVENTS

The International Skiing Federation (FIS) is the official governing body of the Olympic Alpine events. The FIS establishes the rules and format of the competition and sets up the courses. At the XIII Winter Games in 1980, all Alpine races are being held on 4,867-ft (1,483-m) Whiteface Mountain near Lake Placid.

The **downhill** is the most difficult and dangerous competition in Alpine skiing. The object is simply to race down a long, precipitous course as fast as possible. Crouched low to minimize resistance, downhill racers often reach speeds of more than 65 miles (105 km) per hour. According to FIS rules, all competitors must wear crash helmets. One requirement of the course is that skiers must be able to slide continuously from top to bottom without using their poles. The course must be clearly marked by red control gates, and there can be no obstacles or debris. The FIS rulebook gives detailed specifications concerning bumps, ridges, and curves, so as to reduce the risk of serious accident.

The men's downhill course on Whiteface Mountain is 3,028 m (9,935 ft) long, with a vertical drop of 832 m (2,730 ft); the average incline is 27.5°. The women's course is 2,694 m (8,839 ft) long, with a vertical drop of 700 m (2,297 feet) and an average incline of 26°. The names of the sections of both courses are as follows:

MEN'S COURSE

1. Hurricane Alley
2. Lake Placid Turn
3. Sno-field
4. Dynamite Corner
5. Wilmington Turn
6. Niagara
7. Victoria
8. Grand Canyon
9. Broadway
10. Bump #1
11. Times Square
12. Bump #2
13. Gap
14. Ziel Schuss

WOMEN'S COURSE

1. Cloudspin
2. Cloudspin Turn
3. Crossover
4. The Drop
5. Fallaway
6. Chicane
7. Waterfall
8. Grand Central
9. Valvehouse Bump
10. Fifth Avenue
11. Boreen Bump
12. Boreen
13. Ziel Schuss

SAMPLE SLALOM COURSE

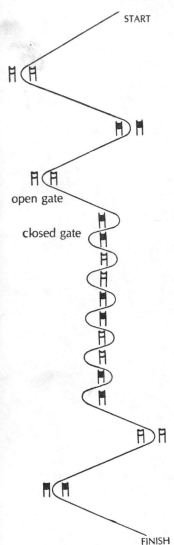

In a slalom run, such as this one, the gates are alternately marked by red and blue flags. Actual gate positions are not set until the day of the competition.

The **slalom** is a race in which skiers follow a steep, twisting course defined by pairs of flags called "gates" *(see accompanying diagram)*. The frequent sharp turns between flags make it a test of stamina and technical skill. The slalom skier must possess quick reflexes, perfect balance, and the ability to concentrate.

Two separate courses will be laid out on Whiteface Mountain for the 1980 competition. Skiers make separate runs on each course, and the final results are based on total time. According to FIS rules, the men's courses must have between 55 and 75 gates, the women's courses between 45 and 60. The gates may be "open" or "closed" *(see diagram)* and must be between 4 and 5 m (13' 1½" and 16' 5") wide. Difficult turns should not be set at the very beginning or end of the course, but the last gates should be fast enough to send the skiers across the finish line "at a good speed." The vertical drop should be between 180 and 220 m (591 and 722 ft) for men, and between 130 and 180 m (427 and 591 ft) for women.

The **giant slalom** is a controlled downhill race. The gates are wider than in the slalom and much farther apart. There must be at least 30 gates in the course, each between 4 and 8 m (13' 1½" and 26' 3") wide. As in the slalom, the gates must be alternately red and blue. The course must be at least 30 m (98' 5") wide, and according to FIS rules, "the terrain should preferably be undulating and hilly."

There are two giant slalom courses on Whiteface Mountain for the 1980 Games—Parkway and Thruway. Each skier makes one run on both courses, and the final standings are determined on the basis of combined time. The two courses are described below:

PARKWAY	THRUWAY
Vertical drop (men): 395 m	**Vertical drop (men):** 395 m
Vertical drop (women): 364 m	**Vertical drop (women):** 364 m
Length (men): 1,301 m	**Length (men):** 1,249 m
Length (women): 1,270 m	**Length (women):** 1,177 m

1. Parkway	1. Mountain Run
2. Thruway Entrance	2. Crossover
3. 1,900 Road Junction	3. Thruway
4. First Lift Crossing	4. Calamity Lane
5. Traverse	5. Burton's Cut-Off
6. Ziel Schuss	6. Ziel Schuss

In all three events, final gate positions are not established until the day of the competition. The skiers are allowed to inspect the course but may not ski through or alongside any of the gates. Their first run through the course may not take place until the competition itself.

A final note on the rules: a skier is not disqualified or penalized for touching or even knocking over a flag, provided he proceeds completely through the gate.

HISTORY

Since its introduction to the Winter Olympics in 1936, Alpine skiing has provided memorable moments for the spectator as well as the competitor. The only Alpine races held that year at Garmisch-Partenkirchen, Germany, were the Combined Events (downhill and slalom) for men and women. Franz Pfnür and Christl Cranz of the host country won gold medals. When the Olympics were resumed in 1948, there were separate slalom and downhill events as well as the combined. Gretchen Fraser's surprise victory in the slalom brought the United States its first medal in skiing. The giant slalom was added to and the combined was dropped from the program in 1952 at Oslo. Andrea Mead Lawrence of the United States won gold medals in the women's slalom and giant slalom, while Austrian and Norwegian skiers dominated the men's competition.

The 1956 Games at Cortina, Italy, were notable for the performance of a 21-year-old Austrian named Toni Sailer. Sailer won the downhill, slalom, and giant slalom by wide margins. Many said his sweep would never be duplicated. Twelve years later in Grenoble, Killy repeated the feat. The only other skier to come close to an Alpine sweep was Rosi Mittermaier, who won the women's downhill and slalom at Innsbruck in 1976, but lost the giant slalom by 0.12 seconds.

Prior to 1980, a total of 50 Alpine skiing events was held at nine Olympic Winter Games. In many cases, the top three finishers were divided by a fraction of a second. While that alone suggests the excitement and intense competition of Olympic skiing, it must be seen to be believed.

A key factor at the 1980 Winter Games will be the quality of the snow. For the first time in Olympic history, the Alpine ski courses will be covered by man-made snow. Aware that differences in consistency and texture require adjustments in technique, several European ski teams have been practicing at U.S. resorts where artificial snow is used. But as long as the snow is white and fluffy, the skiing on Whiteface Mountain in 1980 should be . . . unforgettable.

1980 SUMMARY			
EVENT	**GOLD MEDAL WINNER**	**COUNTRY**	**TIME**
Men's Slalom:			
Men's Giant Slalom:			
Men's Downhill:			
Women's Slalom:			
Women's Giant Slalom:			
Women's Downhill:			

SKIING—Cross-Country

Dates: February 14-15 17-21, 23
Location: Mt. Van Hoevenberg, N.Y.
Number of Events: 8
Held for: men, women

The "Nordic" events of the Olympic Winter Games comprise ski jumping (see *page 27*) and cross-country skiing. The cross-country skier does not barrel down a mountainside at breakneck speed like an Alpine skier but glides across a more level terrain in a rhythmic walking-sliding motion. The skis are narrower and lighter than Alpine skis, and special bindings permit the heel to lift up with every stride. The poles are longer, and the boots are very light, with a flexible sole. The choice of ski wax is important, because the consistency of the snow can greatly slow one's progress. But whatever the conditions, cross-country skiing demands exertion of every part of the body. Sufficient physical conditioning and proper technique are achieved only through long hours of rigorous training.

THE EVENTS

The events for men at the 1980 Games are the 15-km, 30-km, and 50-km individual races, a 4 × 10-km relay, and the Nordic Combined event. The last consists of a 15-km cross-country race and ski jumping competition on the 70-m (230-ft) hill; final standings are based on combined point totals. For women there are 5-km and 10-km individual races and a 4 × 5-km relay.

The rules governing Olympic cross-country skiing are set by the International Skiing Federation (FIS). The courses used in sanctioned competition must be natural terrain. The ground should be altered as little as possible, and man-made obstacles are forbidden. About one third of the course should be uphill, one third downhill, and the rest flat. Overly strenuous hills and monotonous flat stretches should be avoided. All in all, the course should test the skier's stamina and expertise but should not be too difficult or dangerous.

HISTORY

Skiing, like skating, originated in Scandinavia as a means of general transportation and developed into a popular pastime and then a competitive sport. A 5,000-year-old pair of skis on display in a Stockholm museum confirms that skis were in use long before the first ancient Olympic Games. However, formal ski races were not held until the mid-1800's at local carnivals in Norway.

Cross-country skiing was held at the first Olympic Winter Games in 1924. Three events were held that year: the 18 km, 50 km, and Nordic Combined—for men only. Thorleif Haug of Norway won all three gold medals, a feat that has never been duplicated. The program stayed the same until 1936, when the men's 40-km relay was added. Women's competition did not appear until the introduction of the 10 km in 1952. The men's 30-km race and the women's team relay were first contested in 1956, in which year the men's 18-km race was reduced to 15 km.

Norwegians, Swedes, and Finns dominated Olympic cross-country skiing for many years. They won every gold, silver, and bronze medal in men's and women's competition until 1956, when the Soviet Union joined the Winter Games. The Soviets have been especially strong in the women's events. East Germany won several medals in the 1972 and 1976 Games, and Bill Koch's second-place finish in the 30-km race at Innsbruck brought the United States its first cross-country medal.

1980 SUMMARY		
EVENT	**GOLD MEDAL WINNER**	**COUNTRY**
Men's 15 km:		
Men's 30 km:		
Men's 50 km:		
Men's 40-km Relay:		
Men's Combined:		
Women's 5 km:		
Women's 10 km:		
Women's 20-km Relay:		

SKI JUMPING

Dates: February 17, 18, 23
Location: Intervale, N.Y.
Number of Events: 3
Held for: men only

One of the most spectacular and awe-inspiring sights in all of sports is the arched profile of an Olympic ski jumper soaring hundreds of feet through the air, his arms held confidently at his sides, his body leaning forward over the tips of his skis for the greatest possible distance. The grace of the flight is matched only by the skill and balance required to make a steady landing at the bottom of the hill.

Although it is held outdoors in the cold and snow, ski jumping consistently draws the largest crowd of any Winter Olympic event. In February 1980, television cameras are again bringing this dramatic sport into the homes of those who cannot attend in person. The first event is the 70-m (230-ft) special jump on Sunday, February 17. It is called "special" to distinguish it from the 70-m combined jump scheduled for the next day. The latter is part of the Nordic Combined event (*see* Skiing—Cross-Country). The final competition is the 90-m (295-ft) special jump on Saturday, February 23. The 70- and 90-m specifications refer to the distance from the lip of the takeoff to a "critical point" beyond which the hill flattens out and landing becomes difficult.

EQUIPMENT

In addition to skill and confidence, ski jumping requires special equipment. The skis are longer, wider, and heavier than conventional skis, with grooves on the bottom for better control after landing. The bindings are tight with a low hitch at the toes that allows the heel to lift up during the flight. One reason that the sport seems so dangerous is that the ski jumper does not use poles.

SCORING

A common misunderstanding about ski jumping is that the length of the jump is the sole criterion for determining the winner. Although distance is a primary consideration, each jump is also scored for style. It is entirely possible that the man who jumps the farthest will not win the competition. The International Skiing Federation (FIS) has established the stylistic standards that govern Olympic competition. Each contestant begins with a total of 60 style points, 20 from each of three judges. Deductions are then made for stylistic flaws in the flight and landing. These include poor body position, crossing or waving of the skis, touching the snow or skis with the hands, falling, and numerous others. FIS judges are most concerned with faults that endanger the jumper.

The point total for style is then added to the point total for distance. Points for distance are also based on a standard of 60. The full 60 points are awarded to any jumper who reaches a pre-set distance on the hill in question. Deductions are made for every meter that a jumper falls short of the marker. Bonus points are awarded to those who surpass it. In the 70- and 90-m special events, each competitor takes two jumps and the winner is determined on the basis of composite score. In the Nordic Combined competition, each contestant jumps twice from the 70-m hill.

HISTORY

A 70-m ski jumping competition was held at the first Olympic Winter Games in 1924. All three medals went to Norwegian jumpers, with Jacob Tullin-Thams capturing the gold. Norway proceeded to win every Olympic meet until 1956, when Finland came in first and second. The 90-m jump was not added to the program until 1964. The Austrians, East Germans, and Japanese have been especially strong ever since.

The two new jumping hills at Intervale, N.Y. are reputed to be among the best in the world. They were first tested at a pre-Olympic meet in February 1979. Pentti Kokkonen of Finland established himself as a favorite for the 1980 Olympics by winning the 90-m competition and placing second in the 70-m event.

1980 SUMMARY			
EVENT	GOLD MEDAL WINNER	COUNTRY	POINTS
70-m Special:			
90-m Special:			
70-m Combined: See Skiing—Cross-Country			

SPEED SKATING

Dates: February 14–17, 19–21, 23
Location: Olympic Oval, Lake Placid
Number of Events: 9
Held for: men, women

Speed skating is one of several sports that grew out of a means of transportation. Ice skates were first used to cross the frozen lakes, rivers, and canals of northern Europe. As one might expect, many of the world's greatest speed skaters have come from Scandinavia and the Soviet Union. The 400-m (1,312-ft) rink constructed in Lake Placid for the 1980 Olympics is only the second standard-size rink in the United States.

Modern speed skaters remain the fastest self-propelled human beings (on flat terrain) in the world. The speed and excitement of the sport have made it increasingly popular. International competition has gained its greatest impetus from Olympic competition.

RULES AND FORMAT

The rules governing Olympic speed skating are established by the International Skating Union (ISU). In Olympic competition, skaters race against each other two at a time. They skate counter clockwise in separate lanes of an oval track (see diagram). Since the inside lane is shorter than the outside lane, skaters must change lanes every lap at the crossover point. A flagman directs the switch with green and red flags. After all the skaters have completed their run, they are ranked on the basis of fastest time. The blade of a speed skate is normally between 16 and 18 inches (40.6 and 45.7 cm) long, but there are no formal rules regarding its size or construction.

The ISU requires that the races at the Olympics be run in the following order: 500—5,000—1,000—1,500—and 10,000 m for men; and 1,500—500—1,000—and 3,000 m for women. In the men's events, each country may enter four skaters in the 500, 1,000, and 1,500 m and three in the

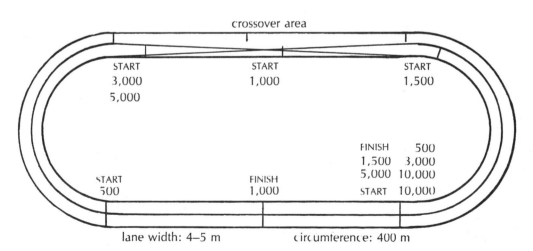

OLYMPIC SPEED SKATING RINK

5,000 and 10,000. However, the total number of entries from each country may not exceed 12. In women's competition, each country may enter three skaters in any event, but the total number of competitors from each team is limited to eight.

Although the supremacy of Soviet and Scandinavian speed skaters has been an Olympic tradition, international competition since the 1976 Games suggests that the United States may put tradition on ice at Lake Placid. In February 1979, Eric Heiden of Madison, Wisc., won his third consecutive world all-around and sprint championships. His sister Beth won the women's overall title and finished second to teammate Leah Poulus Mueller, a silver medalist at Innsbruck, in the sprint championships.

HISTORY

Speed skating was included on the men's program at the first Olympic Winter Games in 1924. That year the 500-m, 1,500-m, 5,000-m, and 10,000-m events were held. The men's program remained unaltered until 1976, when a 1,000-m race was added. In 1932, at Lake Placid, the U.S. team made its best showing. Irving Jaffee (5,000 m and 10,000 m) and John Shea (500 m and 1,500 m) each won two gold medals. The 1932 competition was unique in that the American style of "pack" skating—skating in a group rather than two at a time against the clock—was used for the only time. The Soviet Union sent its first Olympic speed skaters to the 1956 Games at Cortina. Soviet skaters captured three of the four gold medals and established themselves as a world speed skating power. Women's speed skating was first included as an official sport at the 1960 Games. Soviet women have captured 11 of the 20 gold medals awarded in Olympic competition. The most gold medals won by an individual speed skater is six, by Lidia Skoblikova of the USSR in 1960 (2) and 1964 (4).

1980 SUMMARY

EVENT	GOLD MEDAL WINNER	COUNTRY	TIME	OLYMPIC RECORD
Men's 500 m:				:39.17
Men's 5,000 m:				7:22.40
Men's 1,000 m:				1:19.32
Men's 1,500 m:				1:59.38
Men's 10,000 m:				14:50.59
Women's 1,500 m:				2:16.58
Women's 500 m:				:42.76
Women's 1,000 m:				1:28.43
Women's 3,000 m:				4:45.19

FINAL MEDAL STANDINGS

1980 WINTER GAMES

COUNTRY	ABBREVIATION	GOLD	SILVER	BRONZE	TOTAL
Argentina	ARG				
Australia	AUS				
Austria	AUT				
Belgium	BEL				
Bulgaria	BUL				
Canada	CAN				
Chile	CHI				
Czechoslovakia	TCH				
Denmark	DEN				
Finland	FIN				
France	FRA				
German Dem. Rep.	GDR				
Germany	GER				
Great Britain	GBR				
Greece	GRE				
Hungary	HUN				
Iran	IRN				
Ireland	IRL				
Israel	ISR				
Italy	ITA				
Japan	JPN				
Liechtenstein	LIE				
Netherlands	HOL				
New Zealand	NZL				
North Korea	PRK				
Norway	NOR				
Poland	POL				
Rumania	ROM				
Spain	ESP				
Sweden	SWE				
Switzerland	SUI				
USSR	URS				
United States	USA				
Yugoslavia	YUG				
_____	_____				
_____	_____				
_____	_____				
_____	_____				

THE SUMMER PROGRAM

July 19–August 3, 1980
Moscow, USSR

The official program for the XXII Olympic Games in 1980 includes 203 events in 22 sports. This differs from the 1976 program by the following additions: a field hockey tournament for women; two additional weight classes in judo; one new class in weightlifting; and the revival of the 50-km walk. There is a total of 50 events for women only. Yachting, equestrianism, and shooting are the only sports in which men and women compete against each other. A record 12,000 athletes from some 130 nations are expected in Moscow for the Games. Also attending will be approximately 3,500 referees and judges and about 3,500 representatives of the various international sports federations.

At the first modern Olympic Games in 1896 there was a total of 43 events in only 9 sports. For the next several celebrations the program was determined exclusively by the host city. Although the number of medals increased steadily, the choice of sports was rather arbitrary. As international federations for each sport became more organized the situation improved. The International Olympic Committee (IOC) ultimately decided that at least 15 of the following 22 recognized sports had to be included: archery, basketball, boxing, canoeing, cycling, equestrian sports, fencing, field hockey, gymnastics, handball, judo, modern pentathlon, rowing, shooting, soccer, swimming and diving, water polo, track and field, volleyball, weightlifting, wrestling, and yachting. (All 22 are being contested in 1980.)

According to the Olympic charter, only sports that are widely practiced in at least 40 countries and on 3 continents are to be included in the men's program; sports for women must be practiced in 25 countries and on 2 continents. The IOC, in consultation with the international federations concerned, decides which events in each sport shall be included. The IOC also makes the final decision as to how many competitors from each country shall be allowed in a particular event. There are to be 12 entrants in each men's team sport—except for soccer, in which there are 16. For sports in which both men and women participate there are 18 teams, provided that at least 6 of them are women's teams.

The need for such close supervision of the Olympic program is perhaps best explained by the relative obscurity of several sports once included. Among these are: Australian football, budo, jeu de paume, pelota, rackets, and roque. Other sports that have been discontinued are American football, baseball, cricket, croquet, golf, lacrosse, motor boating, polo, rugby, gliding, and tennis. Between 1912 and 1948, competitions also were held in the arts; medals were awarded in such fields as architecture, sculpture, music, painting, and literature. Although formal competitions are no longer held, the *Olympic Charter* still requires that a cultural exhibition be held concurrently with the Games.

Only five nations have participated in all of the 21 Olympic Games since their revival in 1896—Australia, Greece, Great Britain, Switzerland, and the United States. U.S. athletes have brought home by far the greatest number of medals from the Summer Games. The total figures for most medals won are as follows:

	Gold	Silver	Bronze	Total
United States	628	472½	413½	1,514
USSR (formerly Russia)	258	225	207	690
Great Britain	160½	198½	168	527

The most gold medals won by an individual athlete is 10—by Ray Ewry, a U.S. jumper at the 1900, 1904, 1906, and 1908 Games. The most gold medals won by an athlete at one Olympic Games is 7—by Mark Spitz, the U.S. swimmer, at Munich in 1972. The oldest gold medal winner was Sir Eyre Massey Shaw of Great Britain, who won the 2-3 ton class event in the 1900 yachting competition. He was more than 70 years old. The youngest champion is said to be an unnamed French boy who was the coxswain of the winning Dutch rowing pair in 1900. The boy was no more than 10 years old and perhaps as young as 7.

Although the Olympic program has undergone drastic change since 1896, the opening and closing ceremonies remain bound by tradition. The lighting of the Olympic flame in Moscow's Central Lenin Stadium on July 19, 1980, marks the opening of the XXII Games. The competition lasts 16 days, the maximum allowed under Olympic rules. The Games officially end with the extinguishing of the flame on August 3.

THE OLYMPIC SUMMER GAMES

YEAR	SITE	NUMBER OF NATIONS REPRESENTED	NUMBER OF ATHLETES PARTICIPATING
1896	Athens, Greece	13	311
1900	Paris, France	22	1,330
1904	St. Louis, Mo., USA	12	625
1906	Athens, Greece	20	884
1908	London, England	22	2,035
1912	Stockholm, Sweden	28	2,547
1920	Antwerp, Belgium	29	2,607
1924	Paris, France	44	3,092
1928	Amsterdam, The Netherlands	46	3,014
1932	Los Angeles, Calif., USA	37	1,408
1936	Berlin, Germany	49	4,066
1948	London, England	59	4,099
1952	Helsinki, Finland	69	4,925
1956	Melbourne, Australia	67	3,184
1956	Stockholm, Sweden*	29	158
1960	Rome, Italy	83	5,348
1964	Tokyo, Japan	93	5,140
1968	Mexico City, Mexico	112	5,531
1972	Munich, West Germany	122	7,147
1976	Montreal, Canada	88	7,356
1980	Moscow, USSR	130 (est.)	12,000 (est.)

*equestrian events only

ARCHERY

Dates: July 30—August 2
Location: Olympic Complex at Krylatskoye, Moscow
Number of Events: 2
Held for: men, women

Although the bow and arrow have been important in hunting and warfare for many centuries, they likely have been used for recreational purposes for almost as long. Still, the sport of archery had difficulty finding its way onto the Olympic program. A variety of archery contests was held in the Games of 1900, 1904, 1908, and 1920, but the sport did not appear in its present form until 1972.

Olympic archery is governed by the International Archery Federation (FITA). At the Moscow Games, competitions are to be held for men and women. In both events, the archers shoot two FITA International Rounds. Each round consists of 36 arrows shot from four distances. Men shoot from 30 m (98' 4"), 50 m (164'), 70 m (229' 7"), and 90 m (295' 3"); women shoot from 30 m, 50 m, 60 m (196' 9"), and 70 m. The 36 arrows (one "series") at each distance give a total of 144 arrows for the round, 288 for the entire competition. The competitions last four days, with one series shot at two distances each day.

In the FITA round, arrows from the two longer distances are shot at a target 122 cm (48 inches) in diameter; those from the two shorter distances are shot at a target 80 cm (31.5 inches) in diameter. Both targets are divided into five concentric colored rings—gold, red, blue, black, and white from the center outward. Each colored ring is divided in half, yielding zones valued from 1 point to 10 points (bull's eye). The maximum score for one round is therefore 1,440 points; the maximum for each Olympic competition (men's and women's) is therefore 2,880.

Since archery was reinstated as an Olympic sport in 1972, the United States has won all four gold medals. The winners are listed below:

1972 Men: John Williams (USA)   2,528 pts.
      Women: Doreen Wilbur (USA)   2,424 pts.
1976 Men: Darrell Pace (USA)   2,571 pts.
      Women: Luann Ryon (USA)   2,499 pts.

The maximum number of archers from each nation is two men and two women. One man and one woman qualify automatically; a second man may be added if he can score 1,100 points in a preliminary round, a second woman if she scores 1,050. As in the past, the archery fields at Krylatskoye face toward the north. It is customary in international competition that the arrows fly directly in line with the meridian.

1980 SUMMARY

EVENT	GOLD MEDAL WINNER	COUNTRY	POINTS
Men's:			
Women's:			

BASKETBALL

Dates: men—July 20–30
women—July 21–22, 24–25, 27–28
Locations: men—Indoor Stadium on Prospekt Mira, Moscow
women—Central Army Sports Club, Moscow
Number of Events: 2 tournaments
Held For: men, women

Basketball differs from most sports on the Olympic program in that it did not evolve from some other game but was deliberately invented. Although basketball was born and developed in the United States, it is played today in more than 140 nations. And while the United States continues to produce the best amateur and professional players, such countries as the Soviet Union, Yugoslavia, Brazil, and Cuba are every year fielding taller, more skilled, and better coached teams. U.S. domination of Olympic basketball is said to be increasingly in jeopardy.

Tournaments for men and women will be held at the 1980 Games in Moscow. The competition promises to be the best ever, with extensive television coverage. The site of the women's tournament is the Central Army Sports Club, while the men play at the new indoor stadium—the largest in Europe—on Prospekt Mira.

HISTORY

Dr. James A. Naismith, an instructor at the Y.M.C.A. Training School in Springfield, Mass., is credited with inventing the game of basketball. In 1891, seeking a new team sport that could be played indoors, Naismith nailed two peach baskets to the gymnasium balcony and brought together a group of students to try out his idea. It was an immediate success. The game was picked up first by schools and colleges on the East Coast and then across the United States. By 1913, more than 20 million people throughout the world were playing basketball. Although there have been important refinements, the rules laid down by Dr. Naismith in 1891 are basic to the game today.

Basketball first appeared in the Olympics when U.S. athletes gave an unofficial demonstration at the 1904 Games in St. Louis. There was no formal competition until 1936, when 22 teams entered the tournament in Berlin. Beginning in 1936, the United States won seven consecutive championships without losing a single game. The U.S. teams were led by such future professional stars as Bill Russell, K.C. Jones, Oscar Robertson, Jerry West, Jerry Lucas, Bill Bradley, Jo Jo White, Spencer Haywood, and Charlie Scott. The Americans' 64-game winning streak came to an end in 1972 when they lost a highly disputed championship match to the Soviet Union. Although many saw it as the beginning of a new era in Olympic basketball, the United States reclaimed the gold medal in 1976 with an easy final game victory over Yugoslavia, 95-74.

While the United States has long been the dominant force in men's amateur basketball, Soviet teams have established the standard of excellence in women's competition. The USSR's national team, which has not lost a game in 10 years, won the first Olympic basketball tournament for women in 1976. The Soviets were led by 7' 2" (2.18 m), 281-lb (127-kg) center Iuliana Semenova and team captain Nadezhda Zakharova.

RULES

The International Amateur Basketball Federation (FIBA), founded in 1932 and with headquarters in Munich, West Germany, is the official governing body for the Olympic basketball tournament. In addition to establishing the rules of play, the FIBA oversees the pre-Olympic elimination process and thereby determines which teams shall participate at the Games.

The international rules published by the FIBA differ slightly from those commonly used in the United States. One difference is the shape of the free throw lane. In American basketball, the lane is bounded by lines extending at right angles from each end of the free throw line to the baseline. By international rules, the lines extend at a greater angle from the free throw line, thereby creating a wider lane *(see diagram)*. Since no player can remain in the lane (and close to the basket) for more than three seconds, the international specifications take away some of the advantage of the taller players.

REGULATION BALL
circumference: 75-78 cm
weight: 600-650 g

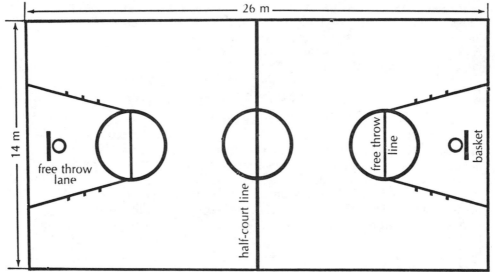

OLYMPIC BASKETBALL COURT

Another feature of international competition is the 30-second rule, whereby a team must attempt a basket within 30 seconds after gaining control of the ball. This has the effect of speeding up the game and creating higher scores; it also bars a team from using stall tactics to protect a lead at the end of a game. Other rules used in international competition that differ from American rules are: 1) when a team is awarded two free throws for a foul, that team has the option of either attempting the shots or taking the ball in from out-of-bounds at the midpoint of a sideline; 2) when a team takes the ball in from out-of-bounds in its own back court, it need not wait for the official to touch the ball; and 3) a timeout may not be called while the ball is officially in play.

These seemingly slight differences between U.S. and international rules are in fact substantial to the players and coaches. U.S. teams must make major adjustments in instinct and strategy in order to succeed in this rough-and-tumble version of the game.

FORMAT

Twelve teams are to participate in the men's tournament in 1980, while six teams are to take part in the women's competition. No more than 12 players are allowed on each team. The host country and the defending Olympic champion qualify automatically. The remaining 10 teams in the men's tournament are determined by zone qualification play-offs. The winners of pre-Olympic tournaments in Europe, Africa, North America, South America, Asia, Oceania, and Central America qualify for the Olympic finals. Losers in the zone qualifications may enter another play-off for the last three spots. The 12 qualifying teams are divided into three groups of four; each group plays a round-robin tournament at the Olympics. The first two teams in each group proceed to the semifinal round, also a round-robin. The first four teams in the semifinals enter the final round; the first- and second-place teams play each other for the gold and silver medals, and third- and fourth-place teams play for the bronze. In the women's tournament, the teams that qualify (five in 1980, because the USSR is both the host country *and* the defending champion) are determined not by zone qualifications but by an open tournament. The six Olympic finalists play a round-robin tournament in Moscow, and medals are awarded on the basis of final standings. No semifinal or final rounds are played.

In 1980, the United States defends its title with the usual array of college stars and a new coach, Bill Gavitt of Providence (R.I.) College. The Soviet Union, with a home court advantage and 7' 4" (2.24 m) center Vladimir Tkachenko, is a strong challenger. With the return of Semenova, their own giant center, the Soviet women's team remains formidable.

1980 SUMMARY

FINAL STANDINGS
(men's)

GOLD:

SILVER:

BRONZE:

CHAMPIONSHIP GAME

TEAMS   FINAL SCORE

FINAL STANDINGS
(women's)

GOLD:

SILVER:

BRONZE:

BOXING

Dates: July 20– 31. August 2
Location: Indoor Stadium on Prospekt Mira, Moscow
Number of Events: 11 weight classes
Held for: men only

Only 75 years ago, the sport of boxing was confined largely to the United States and Great Britain. Since that time it has spread throughout the world, and Olympic medals have been awarded to boxers from such countries as Bermuda, Uganda, South Africa, and North Korea. The most assaulting sport on the Olympic program has done much to promote friendly competition among nations.

HISTORY

Although the art of self-defense was practiced at least 5,000 years ago, boxing as a competitive sport was given its main impetus by the Olympic Games centuries later. Introduced into the Olympics in 686 B.C., boxing eventually spread throughout the Greek and Roman empires and for hundreds of years was a main attraction at the Games. Boxers in the early Olympic era wore headquards and leather straps around their hands for protection. Still, the sport gradually became more brutal and by 30 B.C. was banned by the Romans.

Competitive boxing did not reappear on the scene until the 16th century. Modern technique was greatly influenced by another de-lethalized sport, fencing. James Figg and John Broughton, British heavyweights who made major contributions to the development of boxing in the early 1700's, were also expert fencers. Applying the footwork and defensive tactics of thrust and parry, Figg and then Broughton held the British championship for a total of 32 years.

The first modern Olympics in 1896 did not include boxing because the sport was practiced almost exclusively in the United States and Britain. When it was introduced at the 1904 Games in St. Louis, the United States won every medal in all seven weight classes. The Americans did not send a team to London in 1908, and the British scored a sweep of all five divisions. There was no boxing at the 1912 Olympics in Stockholm because the sport was prohibited by Swedish law.

Interest in the sport continued to grow, and the 1920 Games attracted 118 boxers from 12 countries. The tournament was marred by poor officiating, but the quality of the boxing was high. There were eight weight classes, and three gold medals were won by the United States. More than 180 fighters from 27 countries participated in the 1924 Olympics in Paris. Medals were awarded to representatives of 11 different nations. In this tournament, the referee was stationed *outside* the ring, contrary to modern custom. The result of this experiment was several unfair decisions.

The International Amateur Boxing Association (AIBA), the official governing body of the sport, was founded in 1946 and had a strong positive effect at the London Games two years later. Rules were formalized, incompetent judges and referees were eliminated, and the competition was highly successful with regard to the number of participants and spectators it attracted. The 1952 Games saw the addition of two new weight classes—light welterweight and light middleweight. The light flyweight class was added in 1968, making the 11 now contested.

WEIGHT CLASSES

Elimination tournaments are held in the following 11 weight divisions recognized by the AIBA:

	not	
Light flyweight	exceeding	48 kg (105 lbs 13 oz)
Flyweight	"	51 kg (112 lbs 6 oz)
Bantamweight	"	54 kg (119 lbs)
Featherweight	"	57 kg (125 lbs 10 oz)
Lightweight	"	60 kg (132 lbs 4 oz)
Light welterweight	"	63.5 kg (140 lbs)
Welterweight	"	67 kg (147 lbs 11 oz)
Light middleweight	"	71 kg (156 lbs 8 oz)
Middleweight	"	75 kg (165 lbs 6 oz)
Light heavyweight	"	81 kg (178 lbs 9 oz)
Heavyweight	over	81 kg

Each country is allowed one entry in each weight division, with no reserves. The championship is determined by straight elimination. Although there are only 11 events, 44 medals all together are awarded—a bronze medal is given to the two losing semifinalists in each category.

RULES

The AIBA rules governing Olympic competition place a premium on technique rather than brute strength. While even a gold medalist does not possess the skill or experience of a veteran professional fighter, success at the Olympics is not gained on punching power alone. Speed, accuracy, skillful defense, and respect for the rules are heavily emphasized.

An Olympic bout is three rounds, each three minutes in duration; there is a one minute rest between rounds. The ring must be square, with a minimum length of 16 ft (4.88 m) and a maximum of 20 ft (6.10 m), measured inside the ropes. The boxing gloves each weigh 8 oz (227 g); the leather cannot weight more than 4 oz (113 g) and the padding not less that 4 oz. The knuckle part of the glove, the legal hitting surface, must be marked in a discernible color. The competitors must wear shorts that reach halfway down the thigh and a "vest" that covers the chest and back.

The bout is officiated from inside the ring by an AIBA-approved referee. The contest is scored by five judges seated immediately adjacent to the ring. At the end of each round the judges award 20 points to the "more skillful" boxer and proportionally less to his opponent. Points are awarded on the basis of the number of direct legal hits scored to the head or to the body above the waist. No extra points are awarded for a knockdown. After three rounds, the boxer who has been awarded the decision by a majority of judges is declared the winner. A bout may be terminated earlier if: 1) a boxer retires voluntarily; 2) the referee stops the contest because one of the entrants is injured or "outclassed"; 3) a boxer is disqualified for violating the rules; or 4) there is a knockout. A knockout is recorded when the referee reaches the count of 10 and a fighter is still down. The fallen fighter cannot be "saved by the bell," except in the final round of the championship bout.

Rule 22 of the AIBA rulebook states that contestants must shake hands before the first round and after the announcement of the winner. "Any further shaking of hands between the rounds," the rule reads, "is prohibited."

CHAMPIONS

The only boxer in Olympic history to win three gold medals is László Papp of Hungary, who won the middleweight championship in 1948 and the light middleweight title in 1952 and 1956. O.L. Kirk of the United States is the only boxer to win two gold medals at one Olympics; in 1904 he took the bantamweight and featherweight crowns. U.S. boxers have been the most successful over the years, but the list of winners has a distinctly international flavor. The Eastern European countries have produced numerous champions, and the Cuban team was outstanding in 1972 and 1976.

The list of past Olympic winners also includes numerous fighters who won world professional championships later in their careers. The most easily recognizable names are: Cassius Clay (light heavyweight, 1960); Leon Spinks (light heavyweight, 1976); Joe Frazier (heavyweight, 1964); George Foreman (heavyweight, 1968); and Floyd Patterson (middleweight, 1952).

Teófilo Stevenson, the Cuban heavyweight who won the gold medal in Munich and Montreal, is one of very few Olympic boxers to turn down a professional career. In 1980, his goal is to match Papp's record for the most gold medals. While this might not make him a household name, it certainly would make him one of the greatest amateur fighters of all time. And if it's future professional champions you're looking for, there no doubt will be some in the other weight classes.

1980 SUMMARY

WEIGHT CLASS	GOLD MEDAL WINNER	COUNTRY
Light flyweight:		
Flyweight:		
Bantamweight:		
Featherweight:		
Lightweight:		
Light welterweight:		
Welterweight:		
Light middleweight:		
Middleweight:		
Light heavyweight:		
Heavyweight:		

CANOEING AND KAYAKING

Dates: July 30—August 2
Location: Olympic Complex at Krylatskoye, Moscow
Number of Events: 11
Held for: men, women

The boats used in modern canoeing and kayaking competition are descendants of the birchbark canoe of the North American Indian and the Eskimo hunting kayak. The canoe is an open vessel with a symmetrical convex hull. It is paddled from a kneeling position with a single-blade paddle. The kayak has a top-deck, with holes cut out for each paddler; the paddle itself has a blade at each end.

The Olympic canoeing events are called "Canadian" because of the origin of the craft. The 1980 Games in Moscow include singles (C1) and pairs (C2) competitions at distances of 500 m and 1,000 m. The Canadian events are held for men only. In kayaking, there are singles (K1) and pairs (K2) competitions for men and women. For men, 500-m and 1,000-m races are held in each category; for women, only 500-m races are held. There is also a 1,000-m fours (K4) event for men.

RULES

The rules governing Olympic canoeing and kayaking competition are established by the International Canoe Federation (ICF). The boats themselves can be made of any material; a steering rudder is allowed on the kayak but not on the canoe. Official size and weight specifications for the different craft are as follows:

	K-1	K-2	K-4	C-1	C-2
Maximum Length	520 cm	650 cm	1,100 cm	520 cm	650 cm
	205 in.	256 in.	433 in.	205 in.	256 in.
Minimum Beam	51 cm	55 cm	60 cm	75 cm	75 cm
	20 in.	22 in.	24 in.	30 in.	30 in.
Minimum Weight	12 kg	18 kg	30 kg	16 kg	20 kg
	26.5 lbs	39.7 lbs	66 lbs	36 lbs	44 lbs

For races up to 1,000 m, considered sprints, the course must be straight and in one direction. It is divided into nine lanes, each 7 m (23 ft) wide. The participants draw lots to determine their lane assignments. If the number of entries exceeds nine, preliminary qualifying heats must be held. The race is started by the firing of a gun and the drop of a flag. Lanes are marked by buoys not more than 200 m (656 ft) apart. Competitors must keep strictly within their lanes from start to finish.

Only one boat per country may be entered in each of the 11 events. The maximum number of canoeists and kayakers (men and women) on each team may not exceed 17, including 4 reserves. Although the restriction of one boat per event was intended to increase the distribution of medals among nations, 19 of the 22 gold medals awarded in 1972 and 1976 went to the Soviet Union and East Germany. Two of the other golds went to Rumania; Yugoslavia took the third.

HISTORY

Canoeing and kayaking made their Olympic debuts at the 1936 Games in Berlin. The regatta consisted of 1,000-m races in kayak singles, kayak pairs, Canadian singles, and Canadian pairs; and 10,000-m events in kayak singles, kayak pairs, Canadian pairs, folding canoe singles, and folding canoe pairs. (The folding canoe was a collapsible wooden and canvas kayak.) The 1936 regatta was considered a great success, and the sport was guaranteed a place in future Olympics. The canoeing and kayaking competitions at the 1948 London Games were held on the Thames at Henley. The folding canoe events were dropped from the program, and the 10,000-m Canadian singles for men and 500-m kayak singles for women were added.

Succeeding Olympics saw not only an increase in the number of participating nations, but also further changes in the list of events. Difficulties in building a long course at the 1960 Rome Games led to the elimination of the 10,000-m races. These were replaced by a 4 × 500-m kayak relay for men and a 500-m kayak pairs competition for women. The relay was short-lived, however, as it was replaced in 1964 by the men's 1,000-m kayak fours. A new dimension was added in 1972, when wild-water slalom racing was introduced. Although the event was enormously exciting and popular, the high cost of building artificial courses made it a one-time attraction. The full slate of events planned for Moscow in 1980 is identical to that of 1976.

The record for the most Olympic gold medals in canoeing and kayaking (6) is held by Gert Fredriksson of Sweden. Fredriksson won the 1,000-m kayak singles in 1948, 1952, and 1956; the 10,000-m kayak singles in 1948 and 1956; and the 1,000-m kayak pairs in 1960.

1980 SUMMARY

EVENT	GOLD MEDAL WINNER	COUNTRY	TIME	OLYMPIC RECORD
Men's 500-m Kayak Singles:				1:46.41
Men's 1,000-m Kayak Singles:				3:48.06
Men's 500-m Kayak Pairs:				1:35.87
Men's 1,000-m Kayak Pairs:				3:29.01
Men's 1,000-m Kayak Fours:				3:08.69
Men's 500-m Canadian Singles:				1:59.23
Men's 1,000-m Canadian Singles:				4:08.94
Men's 500-m Canadian Pairs:				1:45.81
Men's 1,000-m Canadian Pairs:				3:52.60
Women's 500-m Kayak Singles:				2:01.05
Women's 500-m Kayak Pairs:				1:51.15

CYCLING

Dates: track—July 22–26; road—July 20, 28
Location: Olympic Complex at Krylatskoye, Moscow
Number of Events: 6
Held for: men only

There is a popular saying in French, *il faut savoir souffrir au vélo,* that means "you have to know how to suffer on a bike." To those who ride a bicycle purely for recreation or transportation, the message is obscure. To anyone familiar with the sport of bicycle racing, however, the meaning is quickly understood. Competitive cycling requires the superb physical conditioning and relentless determination possessed by only the most dedicated and gifted athletes.

THE EVENTS

Modern Olympic cycling consists of two types of competition—**track races** and **road races.** The former are held on a specially constructed indoor track. The track is oval in shape, with back and finishing straightaways. It is banked all the way around. The surface is made of hardwood for traction, and the circumference must be less than 1 km (.62 mi). The newly constructed track at Krylatskoye, site of the 1980 Olympic competition, is 333.33 m (1,093' 8") in circumference, 9 m (29' 6") in width, and made of Siberian larch. The four track events on the 1980 program are the 1,000-m sprint; 1,000-m time trial; 4,000-m individual pursuit; and 4,000-m team pursuit.

The **sprint** race is run over three complete laps of the indoor track. Preliminary heats involve three riders on the track at once, with either two or three on the track during the finals. Starting positions are decided by drawing lots. Although the race covers 1,000 m, only the last 200 are timed. During the first part of the race the cyclists speed up, slow down, and move across the width of the track to gain a good position for the final sprint.

In the **time trial,** also 1,000 m, the cyclist has the track to himself. From a standing start, he covers the distance as quickly as he can. The fastest time determines the winner.

The **individual pursuit** is contested by two cyclists at a time. They start on opposite sides of the track and attempt to overtake each other. The winner of each race is the cyclist who either overtakes his opponent or first reaches his starting point after covering the 4 km (2.5 mi). The elimination round is a time trial, so that the loser of an individual race can still proceed in the tournament on the basis of a fast time. The quarterfinals, semifinals, and finals are pursuit matches proper.

The **team pursuit** is 4 km and follows the same principle as the individual pursuit. Each team is made up of four riders, and two teams compete against each other. The teams line up on opposite sides of the track, with the team leaders on the inside. The race ends when the third man on one team overtakes the third man on the other team or when he crosses the finish line. The elimination procedure is the same as in the individual pursuit competition.

The road races are longer than the track races and are held on a diversified outdoor course. The Moscow Games include an individual road race and a team road race. A special 13.5-km (8.4-mi) course was built at Krylatskoye, next to the indoor track, for these events.

There are no standard distances for the **individual** and **team road races,** but the latter is normally 100 km (62 mi) and the former approximately 175 km (109 mi). A massed start is always used, and the winner is determined solely on the basis of fastest time.

Every nation is allowed a maximum of 15 cyclists. Each cyclist may participate in any of the events. However, only one entry per country is allowed in the three individual track races (sprint, time trial, and pursuit); one team of four cyclists in the team pursuit; one team of four cyclists in the team road race; and four in the individual road race.

HISTORY

Bicycle races were held at the first modern Olympic Games in 1896, but sports historians remain unsure as to the exact form of many of the events. It is certain, however, that the sport has undergone enormous change since that time. One event staged in 1896 was a 12-hour race! The winner, Adolf Schmal of Austria, rode a distance of 314.997 km (195.73 mi).

A sad incident occurred in 1960. A Danish cyclist collapsed during a long-distance race and subsequently died. It was disclosed that he had taken an overdose of drugs prior to the race. As a result, the International Cycling Federation (UCI) became the first Olympic governing body to bring the problem of doping under control.

From the beginning, superior Olympic cyclists came from France, Italy, The Netherlands, Belgium, Austria, and other Western European countries. But because cycling is a professional sport in those countries, many of the most promising cyclists forego the Olympics for more lucrative competition, and the superiority of the Western European nations in the Olympics has gradually waned. Although they continue to win medals, cyclists from the Soviet Union, the Scandinavian countries, and Eastern Europe have had increasing success.

1980 SUMMARY

EVENT	GOLD MEDAL WINNER	COUNTRY	TIME	OLYMPIC RECORD
4,000-m Individual Pursuit:				4:41.71
4,000-m Team Pursuit:				4:21.06
1,000-m Time Trial:				1:03.91
1,000-m Sprint:				
Individual Road Race:				
Team Road Race:				

EQUESTRIAN EVENTS

Dates: July 24–27, 29–August 1, 3
Location: Equestrian Complex at Bitsa Park, Moscow
Number of Events: 6
Held for: men and women

The first equestrian (horsemanship) event in the ancient Olympic Games was a race in which chariots were drawn around an oblong track by four full-grown steeds. For many years chariot racing was a highlight of the Games, with military leaders, kings, and even the Roman Emperor Nero taking part. Although modern equestrian events are quite different from chariot racing, the most successful Olympic riders of the early modern Games were again military officers, nobility, and royalty. It was a tradition that persisted until after World War II. Women were allowed to compete for the first time in 1948. Equestrianism is one of only three Olympic sports (shooting and yachting are the others) in which men and women compete against each other.

The program for the 1980 Olympics includes six events in equestrianism—individual show jumping and team show jumping; individual dressage and team dressage; the individual three-day competition and the team three-day competition. Weather permitting, all the events except team jumping are to be held outdoors at the new equestrian center in Bitsa Park. According to the rules of the International Equestrian Federation (FEI), the team jumping competition must be held in the main Olympic stadium. Following tradition, it will be the last event of the Games before the closing ceremony on August 3.

THE EVENTS

In the show jumping events, horse and rider must jump a series of specially designed obstacles at a specified speed. In the **individual jumping** competition, each nation may enter three riders and horses. The riding is conducted in two rounds, with the final results based on fewest total faults. Faults are assessed according to FEI's "Table A":

First refusal to jump	3 faults
Second refusal	6 faults
Third refusal	Elimination
Obstacle knocked down	4 faults
Fall of horse or rider	8 faults
Exceeding the time limit	¼ fault per second

In the first round there must be 12 to 15 obstacles varying in height from 1.30 to 1.60 m (4'3" to 5'3"). The course may not exceed 1,000 m (3,281 ft). The 20 best riders in the first round take part in the second round. The latter is run over a different course of 10 obstacles. The required speed in both rounds is 400 m (1,312 ft) per minute.

Four riders and horses from each nation compete in the **team jumping** event. This also is conducted in two rounds and judged according to Table A. Participation in the second round is reserved for the eight best teams in round one. Final standings are based on the smallest number of faults for the three best riders on each team in both rounds. Both rounds are held on the same course. There must be 12 to 15 obstacles, varying in height from 1.30 to 1.60 m. The course may not exceed 1,000 m and the required speed is 400 m per minute.

Dressage, the French word for horse training, is the competition that most rigorously tests a horse's poise, obedience, and overall physical development. These qualities are assessed on the basis of a series of required movements—controlled gaits, changes of direction, lateral movements, and the like. Each series of movements is graded from 0 (not executed) to 10 (excellent). Penalty points are deducted for "errors of the course," such as omitting a movement or making a wrong turn. The Olympic dressage competition is run over three days (July 30–August 1, with the **team dressage** held on the first two. The specific test used in this event is called the Grand Prix Special. The winning team is decided on the basis of highest total points.

The **individual dressage** is restricted to the top performers in the Grand Prix Special. The test used in the individual competition is called the Grand Prix. This, according to FEI rules, is intended to bring out "the horse's perfect lightness, characterized by the total absence of resistance and the complete development of impulsion." No horse can take part in either the team or individual dressage that has been trained by anyone other than the competing rider.

The **three-day event** is the most rugged and demanding of the Olympic equestrian disciplines. Horse and rider are tested in three areas—dressage, endurance, and show jumping—in that order. The three parts are held on separate days, but because of the great number of competitors the dressage requires two full days. Thus, the overall competition really takes place over four days (July 24–27). Each nation may enter four riders and horses in the event, of which the best three are counted in the team scoring. In each part of the competition, penalty points are assessed for such flaws as knocking down barriers, refusals, and exceeding the time limit. The winning individual or team is the one with the fewest combined penalty points. The dressage and show jumping aspects of the three-day competition are less complicated and less difficult than the special events in those disciplines. The endurance part of the competition consists of four phases: road, track, steeplechase, and cross-country courses. The road and track courses must be a total of 16 to 24 km (10 to 15 mi) long and covered at a rate of 240 m (787 ft) per minute. The steeplechase course, which is 3,450 to 4,140 m (2.14 to 2.57 mi) long, must be completed at an average speed of 690 m (2,264 ft) per minute. The cross-country run covers 7,410 to 7,980 m (4.6 to 4.9 mi) of varied terrain with natural and man-made obstacles; the course must be completed at an average speed of 570 m (1,870 ft) per minute.

1980 SUMMARY

EVENT	GOLD MEDAL WINNER	COUNTRY
Individual Three-Day Event:		
Team Three-Day Event:		
Individual Dressage:		
Team Dressage:		
Individual Jumping:		
Team Jumping:		

FENCING

Dates: July 22–31
Location: Central Army Sports Club, Moscow
Number of Events: 8
Held for: men, women

The three weapons used in Olympic fencing—**foil, épée,** and **sabre**— have predecessors several hundred years old. The foil is a direct descendant of the short dress sword used in 17th century Europe. It is about 43 inches (109 cm) long and weighs approximately 17 oz (482 g). The foil has a flexible rectangular blade and a blunt point. The épée, which is as long as the foil but heavier and more rigid, is a replica of the old dueling sword. It has a large bell guard, a triangular blade, and the point is covered by a small barbed cone. The sabre used in amateur fencing competition is much like the old cavalry sabre. It has a thin, triangular blade with a dull cutting edge and a blunt point.

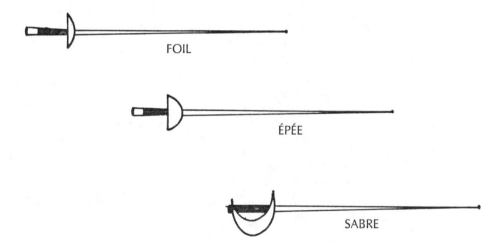

FOIL

ÉPÉE

SABRE

HISTORY

Fencing began to develop as a sport during the 1600's, after guns started to replace swords as the most important battle weapon. Academies appeared all over Europe to instruct gentlemen in the sport of fencing. Foil and sabre events were held at the first modern Olympic Games in 1896. The épée was added in 1900. The first regular Olympic team competition in foils took place in 1904. Sabre and épée teams were added two years later. Women's fencing was begun in 1924 with the individual foil competition. The women's team foil event was added to the program at the 1960 Games.

France, Italy, and Hungary have long histories of success in Olympic fencing. France and Italy won a large majority of all the foil and épée competitions until 1956. Hungary has dominated the sabre events, winning 9 of the first 12 team championships. The USSR has fielded powerful teams since the 1960 Games, especially in women's competition. Soviet fencers have won four of the five gold medals in women's team foil.

Perhaps the greatest fencer in Olympic history was Nedo Nadi of Italy who won an unprecedented five gold medals in 1920—individual foil, individual sabre, and the three team events. Nadi also won an individual championship (foil) in 1912. The only other fencer to win three individual gold medals was Ramón Fonst of Cuba in 1900 (épée) and 1904 (foil and épée). The record for most Olympic fencing medals is held by Edoardo Mangiarotti of Italy, who won a total of 13 golds, silvers, and bronzes between 1936 and 1960. Mangiarotti is one of several fencers to have competed in four or five Olympic Games. Experience and poise are so important that many great fencers do not reach their peak until age 35. Once they have gained sufficient maturity and knowledge of the sport, however, they may fence on the world-class level for as long as 25 years.

RULES

The object in fencing is to touch the opponent with a certain part of the weapon and at the same time avoid being touched. In foil competition, a touch is made only with the point of the blade on the opponent's trunk section. In the épée, a touch may be made on any part of the opponent's body. In sabre, touches are made with either the point or edge of the blade; they may land anywhere above the waist, including the arms and head. Gloves, masks, and protective clothing are worn in all events. Electrical apparatus is used to record touches. Five touches wins a match in the men's events, four in the women's foil.

A country may send up to 16 fencers and two reserves to the Olympic Games. A maximum of three fencers from each nation may be entered in each weapon classification. After qualifying rounds have reduced the pool to 16 or 32 fencers (depending on the original number of entries) in each classification, direct elimination matches are held. Four surviving fencers enter the final round. In the team competition, five fencers may be fielded but only four compete. The tournament normally is conducted on a direct elimination basis.

The governing body for Olympic fencing is the International Fencing Federation (FIE), founded in 1913.

1980 SUMMARY

EVENT	GOLD MEDAL WINNER	COUNTRY
Men's Individual Foil:		
Men's Team Foil:		
Men's Individual Épée:		
Men's Team Épée:		
Men's Individual Sabre:		
Men's Team Sabre:		
Women's Individual Foil:		
Women's Team Foil:		

FIELD HOCKEY

Dates: men—July 20–21, 23–24, 26–27, 29–August 1
women–July 25–26, 28, 30, August 1
Locations: Small Arena, Dynamo Sports Complex, Moscow
Young Pioneers Stadium, Moscow
Number of Events: 2 tournaments
Held for: men, women

Field hockey is probably the earliest ancestor of all the sports in which a ball and stick are used. Polo, cricket, ice hockey, and baseball are all later additions to the family of games that derived from the field hockey played more than 2,500 years ago in Egypt, Persia, and Greece. Today, the popularity of the sport among school-age girls in the United States has given rise to the misconception that it is for women only. To the contrary, field hockey is played by men and women the world over. The first Olympic competition for men was held in 1908. The first tournament for women will take place at the 1980 Games in Moscow.

RULES

Hockey is played by two teams of 11 players each. The object is to hit a hard white ball (*see diagram*) with the face of a stick into the opponent's goal. The team that scores the most goals wins the match. The ball is made of cork and twine covered with leather. The wooden stick can be any length but must weigh between 12 and 28 oz (340 and 794 g) and must be passable through a ring 2 inches (5 cm) in diameter. The flat left side of the head is the only surface that may be used to hit the ball. The game is normally played on a grass pitch (*see diagram*) 100 yds (92 m) long and 55–60 yds (50–55 m) wide. Each goal is 7 ft (2.13 m) high and 12 ft (3.66 m) wide. The "striking circle" in front of each goal measures 16 yds (14.6 m) from the closer goalpost. Balls hit into the goal are counted only if struck within this area.

REGULATION BALL
circumference: 22–23 cm
weight: 155–163 g

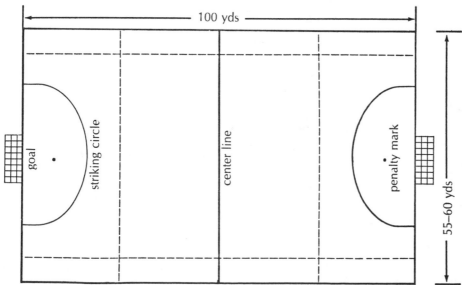

OLYMPIC FIELD HOCKEY PITCH

Each 11-member team consists of 1 goalkeeper, 2 to 4 defensive players called "backs," 3 mid-fielders called "halfbacks," and 3 to 5 attacking "forwards." The number of players at each position and their basic formation are determined by the overall strategy of the team. The trend in recent years had been toward a more defensive alignment with fewer forwards and more backs. The goalkeeper, who wears special protective padding, may kick the ball, catch it with the hands, or stop it with the body. The other players may stop it with hands and stick only.

Olympic field hockey is governed by the International Hockey Federation (FIH). In the 1980 Games, 12 teams will participate in the men's elimination tournament. Six women's teams will play a round-robin.

HISTORY

As the list of past champions shows, India has established a dynasty of sorts in Olympic field hockey. It has captured 7 of the 13 gold medals awarded in the sport.

PAST CHAMPIONS

1908	Great Britain	1952	India
1920	Great Britain	1956	India
1928	India	1960	Pakistan
1932	India	1964	India
1936	India	1968	Pakistan
1948	India	1972	West Germany
	1976	New Zealand	

An important reason for India's winning tradition was its emphasis on offensive skills and strategies. The recent trend toward more defensive formations has therefore diminished India's success. Since 1956, Pakistan has been a formidable rival, capturing 2 gold, 3 silver, and 1 bronze medal. New Zealand was the surprise winner in 1976, with Australia second and Pakistan third. It was the first time since 1920 that India did not win a medal.

1980 SUMMARY

FINAL STANDINGS
(men's)

GOLD:

SILVER:

BRONZE:

CHAMPIONSHIP GAME

TEAMS   FINAL SCORE

FINAL STANDINGS
(women's)

GOLD:

SILVER:

BRONZE:

GYMNASTICS

Dates: July 20–25
Location: The Palace of Sports at Luzhniki, Moscow
Number of Events: 14
Held for: men, women

Gymnastics is one of the most beautiful and physically demanding of all sports. It has been said that a world class gymnast displays more grace, skill, and strength during a one-minute routine than a baseball player or track and field athlete in an entire season.

The gymnastics program at the 1980 Olympics includes 14 events: for men—the pommeled horse, rings, long horse vault, parallel bars, horizontal bar, and floor exercise; and for women—the vault, uneven bars, balance beam, and floor exercise. In addition, competitions are held to determine the men's and women's individual combined (or all-around) champions and the men's and women's team champions.

HISTORY

The sport had its origins in ancient Greece. The word "gymnastics" comes from the Greek *gymnazein*, meaning to exercise naked. These exercises were used primarily for body building and were considered part of the necessary regimen for young men. The beauty and drama of such performances gradually were recognized, and gymnastics emerged as a competitive sport.

The International Gymnastics Federation (FIG), official governing body of Olympic competition, was founded in 1881. That year, The Netherlands, Belgium, and France agreed to invite each other to their respective national meets. Subsequently, other European countries joined this association and contests were held regularly. The FIG, meanwhile, had been actively supporting Baron Pierre de Coubertin's idea of reviving the Olympic Games.

At the first modern Games in 1896, eight gymnastics competitions—parallel bars (individual and team), horizontal bar (individual and team), long horse, pommeled horse, rings, and rope climbing—were held for men only. Some 75 athletes from five countries participated; 60 were from the host country of Greece. The 1900 Games saw the first individual all-around competition, with Gustave Sandras of France taking the championship. In 1904 at St. Louis, the United States won practically every event, including one called "club swinging." Women's gymnastics was not added to the program until 1928, when a women's team event was held. This was the only women's competition until 1952, when medals were awarded in a full complement of individual events.

RECORDS

Over the years, Japan and the Soviet Union have produced many of the world's greatest gymnasts. Japan has won the most team titles in men's Olympic competition, capturing the gold medal in all five Games beginning in 1960. The Soviet Union has won every women's team championship from 1956 on. Several Eastern European countries—

Czechoslovakia, Rumania, Hungary, and East Germany—have also been outstanding.

The most successful male gymnasts have been Viktor Tschukarin of the USSR, who won 7 gold medals, 3 silver, and 1 bronze in 1952 and 1956; and Boris Schakhlin, also of the USSR, who won 7 gold, 4 silver, and 2 bronze in 1956, 1960, and 1964. Among the women, Larissa Latynina of the USSR and Vera Cáslavská of Czechoslovakia were formidable. Latynina holds the all-time record for total number of Olympic medals with 18—6 individual and 3 team gold medals, 5 silver, and 4 bronze in 1956, 1960, and 1964. Cáslavská won 7 individual gold medals and 4 silver medals in 1960, 1964, and 1968. Olga Korbut became the darling of the Munich Olympics in 1972 with superlative performances in the floor exercise and balance beam events. In 1976, Rumania's Nadia Comaneci became the first Olympic gymnast to earn a perfect score of 10.0; she was awarded seven of them.

THE EVENTS

FLOOR EXERCISE MAT

The **floor exercises** are usually held first in a gymnastics meet because they do not require so much strength as some of the other events and therefore give the athletes a chance to warm up. The gymnast performs leaps, somersaults, tumbling, and acrobatic exercises on a padded mat. The entire exercise area should be used, but deductions are made for stepping outside the designated boundaries, shown by the dotted line in the diagram at the left. A routine lasts between 1:00 and 1:30 minutes. Women perform to music, men do not.

BALANCE BEAM

The **balance beam** is a women's event. The gymnast performs leaps, spins, pivots, dance steps, and a variety of exercises on a wooden beam 10 cm (4") wide, 5 m (16' 5") long, and 1.20 m (3' 11") above the floor. According to FIG rules, there must be harmony and dynamic changes, no repetition, a mount and dismount, and few sitting or lying positions. Deductions in score are made not only for falling on the floor or using the hands for support, but even for unnecessary arm or leg movements to maintain balance. The full length of the beam must be used.

PARALLEL BARS

Exercises on the **parallel bars** consist mainly of swinging and vaulting movements, dips, press-ups, and at least one move in which both hands are released from the bars simultaneously. Balance and agility are probably more important than strength in this event. The bars are a maximum of 1.70 m (5' 7") high. Smaller gymnasts are best suited. Competition is held for men only.

In the **uneven** or **asymmetrical bars,** a women's event, the gymnast swings, pirouettes, and somersaults between two bars at different heights—2.30 m (7' 6½") and 1.50 m (4' 11"). It requires grace, creativity, and sheer athletic ability. The rapid changes in grip and direction make it one of the most difficult but most popular events. The dismount, which must be executed from a swinging movement and not from a stationary position, is especially exciting.

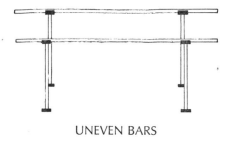

UNEVEN BARS

The **rings** probably requires the greatest strength of all the events and is performed by men only. Hanging from two rings suspended a maximum of 2.5 m (8' 2½") off the ground, the gymnast must swing, perform headstands, and hold at least one static position. An especially noteworthy element is the "cross," in which the gymnast hangs absolutely still with his arms fully extended in a horizontal position. The rings should be still at all times, and the routine must end with the gymnast landing on the floor with both feet together.

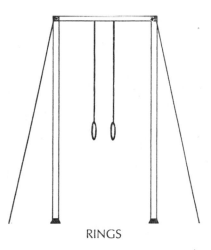

RINGS

Another event that requires great upper-body strength is the **side** or **pommeled horse,** also for men only. The gymnast supports his entire weight by holding either the two pommels (wooden handles) or the leather-covered body of the apparatus. He then begins continuous swinging movements with his legs, executing splits, forward and reverse scissors, and circles. The height of the swing is an important factor in scoring. No part of the foot or leg may touch the horse at any time. The apparatus is adjustable, but the top surface must be set between 1.10 and 1.35 m (3' 7" and 4' 5") above floor level.

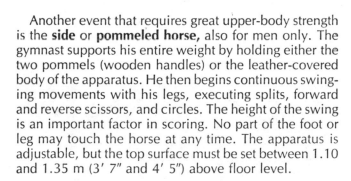

POMMELED (SIDE) HORSE

Men and women gymnasts also use the horse for **vaulting.** For this event the two pommels are removed. The height of the apparatus for men is 1.35 m (4' 5"), for women 1.10 m (3' 7"). The vaulter takes a long running start and jumps off a springboard just in front of the horse. Men go over the full length of the horse, women across the width. The vaulters may touch the apparatus for control before propelling themselves into spectacular turns and twists high above the floor. They must land firmly and steadily on both feet.

The **horizontal** or **high bar** is one of the most exciting events. Two and one-half meters (8' 2½") off the ground, the single steel bar is used for giant swings, counterswings, spins, and acrobatic vaulting dismounts. The chalk that the gymnast uses on his hands may have a great effect on his performance; the wrong type may cause slipping or excessive friction. Only men compete in this event.

HORIZONTAL BAR

FORMAT

The Olympic team championship is determined on the basis of Competitions 1a and 1b in the FIG classification. Competition 1a is the **compulsory** exercise, which is the same for all competitors. Competition 1b is the **optional** exercise, which is composed by the individual gymnast. Six gymnasts from each of 12 teams may participate in the men's and women's championships respectively. The five best scores obtained by each country in each exercise are added together. The team with the highest total wins the Olympic championship.

Competition 2 determines the individual all-around champions. Three participants from each country are allowed in the men's and women's competitions. In this case, only optional exercises are performed. The gymnast with the highest total score for all events (6 for men, 4 for women) is the all-around champion.

Competition 3 determines the individual championship for each event. The top six finishers in each event of Competition 1 qualify for these finals, but there is a limit of two gymnasts per country per event. Again, only optional exercises are performed. Medals are awarded to the best gymnasts in each event (6 for men, 4 for women).

SCORING

In both men's and women's competitions, there are four judges and one head judge. The four judges write their scores independently after every exercise. The highest and lowest of the four are discarded, and the two middle scores are averaged. The score of the head judge is considered only if the difference between the two middle scores exceeds established limits.

Compulsory and optional exercises are scored from 0 to 10.00. Compulsory exercises are rated according to the execution (form and technique) of prescribed elements. Deductions are made for the omission or flawed execution of a particular element. Optional exercises are scored on the basis of three factors: difficulty, composition of the routine, and execution. Bonus points may be awarded for risk, originality, and virtuosity.

Standardized point deductions are made for falls from the apparatus and other flaws in a performance:

Fall from apparatus	0.50 points
Fall during dismount	0.50 points
Fall on or against apparatus	0.50 points
Fall on the knees or seat	0.50 points
Omission of dismount	0.50 points
Unwarranted touching of apparatus	0.10—0.30 points
Stop or hesitation	0.10—0.30 points
Steps or hop after dismount	0.10—0.20 points

TRENDS AND DEVELOPMENTS

Since gymnasts in ancient Greece first engaged in formal competition, the sport has steadily grown more difficult and complex. Modern rules encourage originality and innovation, and the evolution continues to be rapid. Several years ago, the double somersault with a pirouette was considered a difficult floor exercise for any gymnast. Today it is being mastered by 13-year-olds. Meanwhile, Nikolai Andrianov, the men's all-around champion at the 1976 Olympics, and others have performed the *triple* somersault.

Many coaches and critics insist that the sport is becoming too dangerous. The spectacular, airborne moves introduced in recent years—such as Olga Korbut's "loop" on the uneven bars and Nelli Kim's vaulting "Tsukahara with a pirouette"—risk serious injury to both the inexperienced and accomplished gymnast. Still, these elements are being taught to the youngest students of the sport. The new champions are perfecting even more difficult and complex maneuvers. However daring were the routines of Olga Korbut in 1972 and however polished the performance of Nadia Comaneci in 1976, they are likely to be surpassed in 1980. Unless FIG officials change their policies with regard to the awarding of perfect scores, it is likely that several 10's will be given out at Moscow's Palace of Sports.

1980 SUMMARY		
EVENT	**GOLD MEDAL WINNER**	**COUNTRY**
Men's Individual Combined:		
Men's Floor Exercises:		
Men's Horizontal Bar:		
Men's Long Horse:		
Men's Parallel Bars:		
Men's Rings:		
Men's Pommeled Horse:		
Men's Team:		
Women's Individual Combined:		
Women's Floor Exercises:		
Women's Balance Beam:		
Women's Horse Vault:		
Women's Uneven Bars:		
Women's Team:		

HANDBALL

Dates: July 20–30
Locations: men—Sokolniki Sports Palace, Moscow
women—Dynamo Sports Palace, Moscow
Number of Events: 2 tournaments
Held for: men, women

Olympic handball is a team sport gaining popularity throughout the world. It should not be confused with the game played in the United States—properly called Irish handball—in which two players slap a black rubber ball against a wall. Team handball has elements of both basketball and soccer football. The object is to throw an inflated leather ball (*see diagram*) into the opponent's goal. (As in soccer, each goal is worth one point; the team with the most goals wins the match.) The players on each team pass the ball as quickly and as accurately as possible to set up the best shot at the goal. Both the patterns of offense and the techniques of defense are highly reminiscent of basketball.

RULES

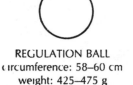

REGULATION BALL
circumference: 58–60 cm
weight: 425–475 g

Team handball can be played either indoors or outdoors. The handball played at the Olympics today is the indoor variety. There are 7 players on a side, including a goalie. Another 5 players may be kept on the team as substitutes. The court (*see diagram*) is considerably smaller than the outdoor playing area.

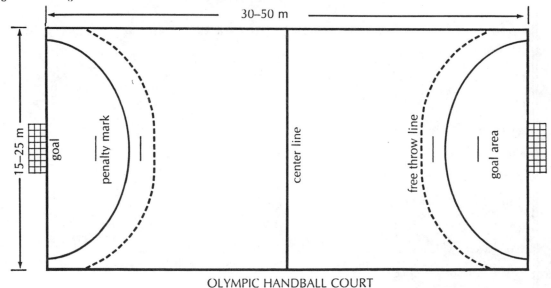

OLYMPIC HANDBALL COURT

The ball is played primarily with the hands but may be touched with any part of the body from the knees up. The goalie may touch the ball with any part of the body, provided he or she is in the designated goal area. No player may hold the ball for more than three seconds or carry it more than three steps. However, as in basketball, a player may dribble the ball while standing, walking, or running.

The game is conducted by two referees, one scorer, and one time-keeper. Play begins from the center point with one team (determined by a coin toss) taking possession of the ball. Shots at the goal, which is 3 m (9' 10") wide, must be taken from outside the goal area. However, the shooter may leap across the line the moment the ball leaves his hand. When the goalie stops a shot, he or she begins the offensive attack by making a "goal throw." During this throw, the opposing players must remain beyond the freethrow line—a broken line 3 m outside the goal area. Since handball is strictly a noncontact sport, it is forbidden to grab, trip, or physically restrain another player. If a defender commits a "serious infringement" of the rules or intentionally enters his own goal area to prevent a goal, a player from the opposing team is given a penalty shot from a distance of 7 m (22' 11½"). In men's competition a match is normally two periods of 30 minutes each. A women's match is normally two 25-minute periods.

At the 1980 Olympics, tournaments will be held for men and women. Twelve teams will take part in the men's competition, six in the women's.

HISTORY

Team handball was introduced into the Olympics at Berlin in 1936. A men's tournament of outdoor handball was held, and Germany took the gold medal. An exhibition tournament was held in 1952 at the Helsinki Games. The sport was reintroduced in 1972 with an indoor tournament for men. Eastern European teams showed their superiority; Yugoslavia, Czechoslovakia, and Rumania finished first, second, and third, respectively. A women's tournament was added in 1976. The Soviet Union came in first, with East Germany and Hungary the runners-up. The Soviet men's team also went away with a gold medal in 1976, as Rumania took the silver and Poland the bronze.

1980 SUMMARY

FINAL STANDINGS
(men's)

GOLD:

SILVER:

BRONZE:

CHAMPIONSHIP GAME

TEAMS   FINAL SCORE

FINAL STANDINGS
(women's)

GOLD:

SILVER:

BRONZE:

JUDO

Dates: July 27—August 2
Location: The Palace of Sports at Luzhniki, Moscow
Number of Events: 8 weight classes
Held for: men only

Judo, which means "soft" or "easy way" in Japanese, is a weaponless combat sport in which the contestants employ specialized principles of movement, balance, and leverage to 1) throw the opponent to the ground, 2) hold the opponent with his back on the ground, 3) strike or apply pressure to the opponent's joints and sensitive areas, or 4) choke the opponent until he resigns or is rendered unconscious. The underlying concept of judo is that a combatant can be most effective by giving way to the attacking force. He uses the opponent's own movements to put him off balance and throw him to the ground.

Judo is a refined version of the ancient martial art of jujitsu. It was developed in Japan in the late 19th century but has since developed sufficient international popularity to be included in the Olympic Games. In 1980, competition will be held in eight weight classes, two more than in 1976. The classification system of 1976 was changed so as to include the following divisions: not exceeding 60 kg (132 lbs 4 oz); 65 kg (143 lbs 5 oz); 71 kg (156 lbs 8 oz); 78 kg (171 lbs 15 oz); 86 kg (189 lbs 10 oz); 95 kg (209 lbs 7 oz); over 95 kg; and an open class.

RULES AND REGULATIONS

Judo matches (shiai) are held on a square mat made of compressed straw with a canvas cover. The contest area is a minimum of 9 m (29' 6") and a maximum of 10 m (32' 10") on each side. This is surrounded by a safety area 1 m (3' 3") wide. The bout is supervised by a referee, who remains inside the contest area, and two assisting judges. The combatants (judoka) must wear a special judo costume (judogi), which consists of a loose-fitting jacket and trousers with no buttons or pockets. No shoes or socks are worn.

The contest is begun with the two fighters facing each other at the center of the mat. After they bow, the referee pronounces hajime (begin) to start the match. Most of the fighting takes place in the contest area, but a fighter may be thrown into the safety area if his opponent is completely inside the contest area when he begins the movement. The winner of the bout is determined on the basis of throwing techniques (nage-waza) and grappling techniques (katame-waza). A contest is normally scheduled for 5–7 minutes but is immediately stopped when one of the participants gains a decisive advantage, as outlined below. If the time limit elapses and no fighter has gained a decisive advantage, the victory is awarded to the more skillful competitor.

During the course of a bout a fighter is rewarded for successfully executing a movement or hold but penalized for any infringement of the rules. The degree of the reward depends on the specific hold or throw executed, and the severity of the penalty depends on the seriousness of the infringement. The referee awards an ippon (full point) and stops the bout when one fighter takes complete advantage in one of several ways:

throws the opponent on his back with appreciable force; holds the opponent on his back for 30 seconds; applies a lock or strangle hold with "sufficiently apparent effect"; or forces the opponent to resign. The next highest advantage declared by the referee is the *waza-ari* (near ippon). Should a fighter gain a waza-ari plus some other advantage, the bout is stopped and he is declared the winner. Fractions of a point are awarded for a *yuko* (near waza-ari) *koka* (near yuko), and *osaekemo* (holding), but the bout will not be stopped unless there is also an ippon or waza-ari.

The penalties for infringement of the rules are either slight *(shido)*, moderate *(chui)*, serious *(keikoku)*, or very serious *(hansoku-make)*. The specific acts in each category include "adopting an excessively defensive attitude" (slight), applying a leg scissors (moderate), applying a hold which might injure the neck or spine (very serious), and intentionally falling backward onto the opponent (very serious). Very serious infringements are penalized by disqualification.

FORMAT

A maximum of one judoist per country is allowed in each weight class. However, a fighter who has competed in any of the specified weight classes may also compete in the open class. The contestants in each division are grouped into two pools by the drawing of lots. The fighters in each pool are paired off, and matches proceed on a single elimination basis. The winners of each pool then fight each other for first and second place. All contestants in each pool who lost their elimination bouts to the eventual winner of that pool fight each other for third place; two bronze medals are awarded, one for each pool.

HISTORY

Olympic judo competition was first held at the Tokyo Games in 1964, when the host country was allowed to include a sport of its own choosing. To the surprise of no one, Japanese fighters took the gold medal in three of the four weight classes. There was no judo at the 1968 Games in Mexico City, but the 1972 program included competition in six weight classes. Although Japan won three gold medals, its supremacy in the sport had begun to wane. It was a trend that continued in 1976, when Soviet judoists mounted a strong challenge and won two gold medals, two silvers, and one bronze.

1980 SUMMARY		
WEIGHT CLASS	GOLD MEDAL WINNER	COUNTRY
60 kg:		
65 kg:		
71 kg:		
78 kg:		
86 kg:		
95 kg:		
over 95 kg:		
Open:		

MODERN PENTATHLON

Dates: July 20–24
Location: Sites of the five individual sports
Number of Events: 2 (five sports each)
Held for: men only

The modern pentathlon—not to be confused with the similarly named track and field event for women—is a five-day competition in riding, fencing, shooting, swimming, and running. This somewhat odd combination was the idea of Baron Pierre de Coubertin, father of the modern Olympics. Coubertin felt that it would be a more genuine measure of athletic versatility than the decathlons and pentathlons included on the track and field program.

The five events that make up the modern pentathlon were not arbitrarily selected. The event was intended to recreate the ordeal of an imagined military courier who is dispatched on horseback, ambushed and forced to fence with and shoot at his assailants, swim across a river to escape capture, and run some distance to deliver his message. At the Olympics, the five sports are contested on a one-per-day basis in exactly that order. Individual and team competitions are held.

FORMAT AND SCORING

The rules and regulations for the Olympic modern pentathlon are established by the International Modern Pentathlon and Biathlon Union (UIPMB). At the 1980 Olympics, not more than four persons, including one reserve, are allowed from each country. The same three pentathletes who participate in the individual competition also take part in the team contest. Winners are determined on the basis of an elaborate point system, described below. The pentathlete with the highest combined score for the five events wins the individual gold medal. In the team competition, medals are awarded on the basis of the aggregate score of all three team members. The point system is constructed so as to favor pentathletes with equal competence in all five sports and to penalize those who are strong in some but weak in others.

The first competition is **riding.** This was originally a cross-country race but was later changed to a form of show jumping. The course is 800 m (2,625 ft) long, with 15 obstacles (including one double jump and one triple jump). Riders who complete the course without fault in 4 minutes receive 1,100 points. Points are deducted for knocking down barriers, swerving or refusing to jump, falling, and exceeding the time limit.

The **fencing** competition is a round-robin tournament of one-touch bouts in épée. The duration of each bout may not exceed 3 minutes. The fencer who wins 70% of his bouts is awarded 1,000 points. Points are gained or lost for bouts above or below the 70% level. They are computed on the basis of the following formula: $\pm\ 11 \times {}^{100}/_a$ where "a" stands for the total number of bouts.

In **shooting,** competitors fire a pistol at a target 25 m (82 ft) away. The target is divided into concentric circles with point values of 0 to 10 inward. Twenty shots—in four series of five—are fired. A score of 194 earns 1,000 points. For every unit above or below 194, 22 points are added or deducted.

The fourth pentathlon event is 300-m freestyle **swimming.** The competition is held in heats, with no finals. A time of 3 minutes 54 seconds earns the swimmer 1,000 points. For each half-second above or below that time, four points are deducted or added.

The last day's event is cross-country **running.** The course covers 4,000 m (2.5 mi), and a time of 14 minutes 15 seconds is rewarded with 1,000 points. Three points are added or deducted for every second below or above that time.

According to this scoring procedure, a total of 5,000 points is considered extremely high for an individual pentathlete. The gold medalist at the 1976 Games, Janusz Pyciak-Peciak of Poland, scored a total of 5,520 points for the five sports. In the team competition, a total of 15,000 points for the three participating athletes is recognized as a fine performance. Great Britain, which won the event in 1976, did so with a point total of 15,559. However, comparing the scores of past Olympics can be somewhat misleading. Standards for the awarding of points have changed considerably, even over the past 15 years.

HISTORY

The modern pentathlon is unique in that it is the only Olympic sport ever to be governed by the International Olympic Committee (IOC). From 1912, when the event was introduced to the Games, until 1948, when the UIPMB was founded, the rules were formulated and administered by a special sub-committee of the IOC. The team event was added to the program for the 1952 Olympics at Helsinki. In 1956, the scoring system was changed from one based on final standings in each sport to the one in present use. And for the 1968 Games, the riding competition was changed from cross-country to jumping.

Because of tradition and the availability of appropriate training facilities, the military services have provided many of the world's best modern pentathletes. At the 1912 Olympics, a young U.S. Army officer named George Patton placed fifth in the modern pentathlon, behind four Swedes. Swedish pentathletes have taken home 9 of the 14 gold medals awarded in the individual event. Hungary also has been strongly represented, capturing three individual and three team championships since the 1952 Games.

1980 SUMMARY			
EVENT	GOLD MEDAL WINNER	COUNTRY	POINTS
Individual:			
Team:			

ROWING

Dates: July 20–27
Location: Olympic Complex at Krylatskoye. Moscow
Number of Events: 14
Held for: men, women

Rowing is one of the most diversified and widely contested sports on the Olympic program. It is surpassed only by track and field and swimming in terms of number of events held (14, and total number of athletes allowed from each country (68). At the XXII Olympic Games in Moscow there are 8 rowing and sculling events for men, 6 for women. Women's competition was held for the first time in 1976.

In **rowing,** each oarsman pulls a single oar with both hands. There are either two, four, or eight oarsmen in the boat. In certain events there is also a coxswain, whose job it is to steer the boat and pace the rowers. The men's program includes coxed pairs, coxless pairs, coxed fours, coxless fours, and (coxed) eights. For women there are coxless pairs, coxed fours, and (coxed) eights. **Sculling** is the art of rowing with two shorter oars (called sculls), one in each hand. Single, double, and quadruple scull races are held for both men and women. All men's races cover a distance of 2,000 m (2,187 yds); the women's races are 1,000 m (1,094 yds).

THE EVENTS

Probably the most difficult event on the program is the **single sculls.** The boat responds to the slightest touch of the blades, and an even, steady stroke is therefore essential. The size of the boat varies with the weight of the sculler; the average length is about 26 ft (7.9 m). The next most difficult event is the **coxless pairs.** Since there is only one oar on each side of the boat, anything less than perfect timing will adversely affect speed and direction. The average length of the shell is about 32 ft (9.8 m). The **coxless fours** is probably next in point of difficulty. The boat is some 39 ft (11.9 m) long and has a small rudder for steering. Since there is no coxswain, the oarsman at the bow of the boat usually steers. He does so with his right foot, which is connected to the rudder by lines running through pulleys inside the boat. The boat used in **double sculls** is the same as the one used in pairs rowing, except that it has two oars at each seat. Perfect timing and uniformity in the length and pressure of each stroke are the goals of the scullers. The **coxed pairs** and **coxed fours** have the advantage of a coxswain to steer the boat and pace the rowers. However, the weight of an additional person creates a heavier drag and more work for each oarsman. The **quadruple sculls**—coxed for women, coxless for men—is a new event. It was added to the schedule at the 1976 Games in Montreal. The **eights** is probably the best known of all the rowing races. It is the fastest and most enjoyable to watch. The sight of eight men pulling together with all their strength and coordination is one of the most beautiful in all of sports. The eight is always steered by a coxswain, who sits in the stern section of the boat. The shell is approximately 60 ft (18.3 m) long.

A racing boat is equipped with outriggers (oarlocks extended outside the boat on metal rods) for better leverage. In rowing there is one outrigger per seat, in sculling two. The seat itself slides forward and back, enabling the oarsman to increase the length of each stroke. The sliding seat also shifts the rower's main source of power from his back to his legs. Watermanship, the skill of balancing the boat and handling the oars, is an all-important skill. At the end of each stroke, every oar must be turned so that the blade rests parallel to the surface of the water; this technique, called feathering, greatly reduces wind resistance. The speed of a boat is determined primarily by the rate and power of the strokes. The pace is altered according to the circumstances of the race and the strength of the crew. In an eight, the heaviest oarsmen usually sit in the middle and the best rowers in the stern.

RULES AND FORMAT

Olympic rowing and sculling competition is governed by the International Rowing Federation (FISA). The FISA has established the order of events for men and women. The men's races are held as follows: coxed fours, double sculls, coxless pairs, single sculls, coxed pairs, coxless fours, quadruple sculls, and eights. The order of events for women is coxed fours, double sculls, coxless pairs, single sculls, quadruple sculls, and eights. Not more than one boat per country may be entered in each event, but each team is allowed several reserves.

An important feature of the elimination procedure is the repechage, whereby losing boats in preliminary heats are given a second chance for the finals. The championship race is held on a six-lane course.

1980 SUMMARY				
EVENT	**GOLD MEDAL WINNER**	**COUNTRY**	**TIME**	**OLYMPIC RECORD**
Men's Coxed Fours:				6:31.85
Men's Double Sculls:				6:47.50
Men's Coxless Pairs:				6:53.16
Men's Single Sculls:				7:10.12
Men's Coxed Pairs:				7:17.25
Men's Coxless Fours:				6:24.27
Men's Quadruple Sculls:				6:18.65
Men's Eights:				5:57.18
Women's Coxed Fours:				3:45.08
Women's Double Sculls:				3:44.36
Women's Coxless Pairs:				4:01.22
Women's Single Sculls:				4:05.56
Women's Quadruple Sculls:				3:29.99
Women's Eights:				3:33.32

SHOOTING

Dates: July 20–26
Location: Shooting Range near Mytishchi (Moscow suburb)
Number of Events: 7
Held for: men and women

Although shooting seems to offer the casual spectator little of the action or excitement of track and field, gymnastics, or skiing, there is no other sport on the Olympic program in which the contestants perform closer to perfection and in which the slightest lapse will have a more detrimental effect. The drama is pure, the pressure on each shooter unrelenting. Lanny Bassham, the U.S. Army captain who won a gold medal in small bore rifle shooting at the 1976 Games, describes the sport as "controlled nonmovement," requiring unique skill and training. Says Bassham:

"If the angle of error at the point of the barrel is more than .005 of a millimeter, you drop into the next circle and lose a point. So we have to learn how to make everything stop. I stop my breathing. I stop my digestion by not eating for 12 hours before the competition. I train by running to keep my pulse around 60, so I have a full second between beats. . . . You do all of this and you have the technical control. But you have to have some years of experience in reading conditions: the wind, the mirage. Then you have the other 80% of the problem—the mind."

Seven shooting events are scheduled for the 1980 Olympic Games in Moscow—free pistol; rapid fire pistol; moving target; small bore rifle, prone; small bore rifle, three positions; international clay pigeon shooting; and skeet shooting. A description of each event, with rules and scoring procedure, is given below. All events are open to men and women. In 1976 Margaret Murdock became the first woman to win an Olympic medal in shooting, when she placed second to teammate Bassham in the three position rifle event.

THE EVENTS

The rules for Olympic shooting are established by the International Shooting Union (UIT). Not more than 14 shooters are allowed on each team, with a maximum of two in each event.

There are two pistol competitions held at the Olympics. The **free pistol,** in which 60 single shots are fired at a target 50 m (164 ft) away, requires the greater precision of the two. The target consists of 10 rings, with point values of 0 to 10 inward; the bull's eye is 5 cm (2 inches) wide. The competition is divided into two parts, each consisting of 10 practice shots and 30 competition shots. The full course must be completed in 2 hours and 30 minutes. The pistol is .22 caliber (5.6 mm); only open sights are permitted. In **rapid fire pistol,** a total of 60 shots is fired at five targets 25 m (82 ft) away. The target is different from the one used in free pistol, with an oval bull's eye 10 cm (4 inches) × 15 cm (6 inches). The competition is divided into two courses of 30 shots, held on separate days. Each course is subdivided into six series of 5 shots; in each series, one shot is fired at each target. Two series must be shot in 8 seconds, two in 6 seconds, and two in 4 seconds. A .22-caliber pistol, weighing a maximum of 1,260 g (2.8 lbs), is used.

Moving target shooting, a rifle event reminiscent of the running wild boar competition held in 1900, was added to the Olympic program in 1972. The target moves at two different speeds and is divided into rings with point values of 0 to 10. Sixty shots are fired over a period of two days. On the first day, 20 shots are fired at each speed of the target; on the second day, 10 shots are fired at each speed. The distance is 50 m.

In two of the seven Olympic shooting events, a **small bore rifle** (.22-caliber rimfire) is used. Telescopic sights are not permitted. Shots are fired from 50 m at a ringed target with a 10-point bull's eye. In the **prone** event each competitor fires 60 shots. There is a time limit of 120 minutes for completing the full course. In the **three positions** competition, a total of 120 shots is fired—40 from a prone position, 40 from a standing position, and 40 from a kneeling position. There is a time limit of 90 minutes for completing the prone series, 120 minutes for the standing series, and 105 minutes for the kneeling series. The changeover between positions may not exceed 15 minutes.

The two shotgun events in the Olympics are **international clay pigeon** (or trench) **shooting** and **skeet shooting.** In both, clay disks are sprung into the air by mechanical traps. The regulation disk is 110 mm (4.3 inches) in diameter and weighs 105 g (3.7 oz). In both events, 200 targets are shot over a three-day period. Three series of 25 are shot on the first day, three series on the second day, and two series on the third day. The shooter who hits the greatest number of targets is the winner. Any type of shotgun, 12-gauge or smaller, may be used. The differences between the events are the design of the shooting range, the number of traps, and the direction in which the targets are flung. In international clay pigeon competition (as distinct from American trapshooting), there are 15 traps set up in a roof-covered trench. These traps propel the targets in random directions at irregular intervals. In skeet shooting, two traps—the "high house" and "low house"—are set up at opposite ends of a semicircular range. Eight firing stations are located on the perimeter of this semicircle. The shooter fires from each station at targets emitted from the high house and low house.

1980 SUMMARY

EVENTS	GOLD MEDAL WINNER	COUNTRY	POINTS	OLYMPIC RECORD
Free Pistol:				573 pts.
Rapid Fire Pistol:				597 pts.
Moving Target:				579 pts.
Small Bore Rifle, Prone:				599 pts.
Small Bore Rifle, 3 Positions:				1,166 pts.
Clay Pigeon (Trench) Shooting:				199 pts.
Skeet Shooting:				198 pts.

SOCCER

Dates: July 20–25 27. 29; August 1–2
Locations: Moscow—Central Lenin Stadium at Luzhniki
Dynamo Stadium
Leningrad—Kirov Stadium
Kiev—Central Republican Stadium
Minsk—Dynamo Stadium
Number of Events: 1 tournament
Held for: men only

Soccer, or "football" as it is usually referred to outside the United States, is justifiably called the world's most popular sport. The game is played almost everywhere under the same basic rules. European and South American countries perennially field the best teams. That soccer continues to gain popularity is evidenced by the number of nations participating in recent Olympic tournaments. To qualify for the final round of play at the Rome Games in 1960, 52 teams participated in the elimination process (described below). The number increased to 90 for the Montreal Games 16 years later.

The Olympic tournament itself has done much to promote the growth of the sport. The event is second only to the World Cup tournament in terms of importance and fan appeal. But while the World Cup typically sees the best play, Olympic soccer has helped develop and popularize the sport in countries just beginning to take part in international competition. Young players are given an opportunity to develop their skills and take part in major international matches.

HISTORY

Although football games can be traced at least as far back as ancient Rome, the modern game of soccer did not develop until the mid-19th century. The London Football Association codified rules and became the governing body for Great Britain in 1863. The sport is still known as ' association football'' in the Commonwealth countries, and the term ' soccer'' is a shortened version of that name.

Soccer was added to the Olympic program for the 1900 Games in Paris, and Great Britain won the tournament. The British also captured gold medals in 1908 and 1912. Still, the greatest success in Olympic soccer belongs to Hungary, which also won three championships (1952, 1964, and 1968) as well as one silver and one bronze medal. Uruguay has twice won the tournament, and 11 other countries have won once. Since 1948, Olympic soccer has been dominated by the Eastern European countries.

PAST CHAMPIONS

1900	Great Britain	1936	Italy
1904	Canada	1948	Sweden
1906	Denmark	1952	Hungary
1908	Great Britain	1956	Soviet Union
1912	Great Britain	1960	Yugoslavia
1920	Belgium	1964	Hungary
1924	Uruguay	1968	Hungary
1928	Uruguay	1972	Poland
	1976	East Germany	

The United States fielded its first Olympic soccer team in the 1924 Games; it was eliminated in the second round. Soccer was not included in the Los Angeles Games of 1932 because most countries could not afford the transportation expenses for so large a team. Italy captured the 1936 gold medal by defeating Austria, 2-1, in an exciting overtime match. The USSR, which won the soccer championship in 1956, made its first appearance in 1952 at Helsinki; 24 other nations entered the tournament that year. Regional elimination trials to determine the 16 finalists were introduced in 1960. A rule barring World Cup players from the Olympics also was introduced in 1960.

RULES AND FORMAT

The International Federation of Association Football (FIFA), founded in 1904, is recognized by the International Olympic Committee (IOC) as the official governing body of Olympic soccer competition. As such, it is responsible for establishing the number of participating countries, devising and overseeing the elimination process, establishing the rules and regulations of play, and determining the eligibility of players.

The game is played on a field—sometimes called a "pitch"—100 to 130 yds (91 to 119 m) long and 50 to 100 yds (46 to 91 m) wide. There are 11 players on a side, including one goalie. The goalie is the only player who may touch the ball with his hands. The others attempt to advance it up the field by passing it primarily with their feet. The object is to shoot the ball into the opponent's goal, which is 8 yds (7.3 m) wide. If a defending player commits a foul or touches the ball with his hands inside his own "penalty area," a player from the opposing team is awarded a free kick at the goal from the penalty mark 12 m (13 yds) away. Olympic soccer matches last a total of 90 minutes—two 45-minute halves—with a five-minute interval. In the semifinal and final rounds of the tournament, a tie score at the end of regulation time is settled by a 30-minute overtime period.

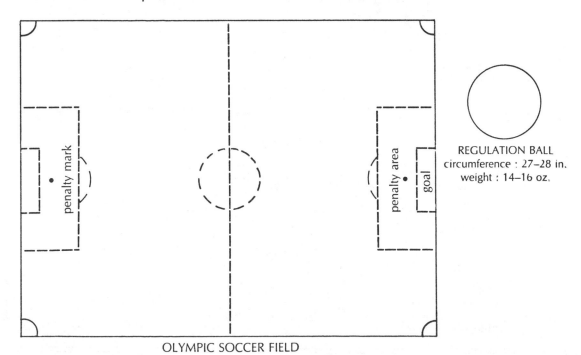

penalty mark

penalty area

goal

REGULATION BALL
circumference : 27–28 in.
weight : 14–16 oz.

OLYMPIC SOCCER FIELD

Following what has become a sort of Olympic tradition, the final elimination rounds in 1980 are to be held in several cities—Moscow, Leningrad, Kiev, and Minsk. The championship match and the match for third and fourth place are scheduled for the main Olympic stadium at Luzhniki, Moscow.

The Amateur Committee of FIFA has worked out an elaborate procedure for determining the 16 teams to participate at the Olympics. East Germany and the Soviet Union qualify automatically, the former by virtue of winning the gold medal in 1976 and the latter because it is the host country. The other 14 entries come from five continents: four from Europe, three from Africa, three from Asia and Oceania, two from South America, and two from North and Central America and the Caribbean. Selections are based on play-off competition. (Interestingly, this format provides for a total of six teams from Africa and Asia, as opposed to one team from each in the world championships.) The 16 entries (each with a 17-man roster) are divided into four groups and are scheduled to play a total of 24 matches, July 20 to 25, in the four Soviet cities. The two top teams in each group proceed to the quarterfinal round, and the best four then go on to the semifinals. The two losing teams from the semifinals will meet August 1 for the bronze medal. The two winning teams face each other for gold and silver the next day.

The problem of preserving amateurism in the Olympics has been especially difficult in the case of soccer. The rule barring World Cup players remained in force until 1968, when it was abolished by the FIFA Congress. But in February 1978, the FIFA Executive Committee passed a resolution again prohibiting World Cup participants from playing in the Olympics. In May, the FIFA Congress adopted a compromise rule: the ban would apply only to players from Europe and South America. And in January 1979, this decision was accepted by the IOC. As a result, many players (including past medal winners) are not competing in 1980. Still, the FIFA ruling was intended to enhance the parity among teams and to help assure a more exciting, wide open tournament.

1980 SUMMARY

CHAMPIONSHIP GAME

TEAMS   FINAL SCORE

FINAL STANDINGS

GOLD:

SILVER:

BRONZE:

SWIMMING AND DIVING

Dates: swimming—July 20–26; diving– July 26–29
Location: Olympiisky Sports Center, Moscow
Number of Events: 30
Held for: men, women

The Olympic swimming and diving competition is like a track meet in water. The program includes 30 events as diverse as springboard diving and the 400-m individual medley. There are sprints, middle and long distance races, and relays. In terms of the total number of medals awarded at the Games, swimming and diving is second only to track and field. Because of the stiff competition, excellent facilities, and emotional buildup, the Olympics provide an ideal setting for record-breaking performances.

THE EVENTS

There are 26 swimming events on the 1980 Olympics program. Races are held in four different strokes at several different distances.

Five **freestyle** events (4 individual and 1 team) are held for both men and women. The men swim 100-, 200-, 400-, and 1,500-m individual races, as well as a 4 × 200-m team relay. The women swim 100-, 200-, 400-, and 800-m races, and a 4 × 100-m relay. Swimmers normally use the "crawl" because it is the fastest stroke. The crawl is executed face down with the body prone on the surface of the water. The arms operate in an alternating pulling motion. A "flutter-kick"—short, alternating, up-and-down kicks—is used.

There are two **backstroke** events—the 100 m and 200 m—for both men and women. The backstroke is an upside-down crawl with the swimmer lying on his back. Again, the alternate-arm stroke and flutter kick are used.

There are two **breaststroke** events—100- and 200-m races—for both men and women. The breaststroke differs from the crawl in that the arms and legs work simultaneously and remain in the water at all times. The swimmer is on his breast, with his shoulders level at the surface. The arms move together from full forward extension, back to the chest, and out again. The legs are drawn up together with a distinct bend in the knees and kicked outward and back in a frog-like motion.

The 100- and 200-m **butterfly** events are held for men and women. The butterfly is a faster variety of breaststroke in which the swimmer seems to lunge forward out of the water. Both arms are flung ahead to full extension, pulled through the water back to the thighs, and thrown out again to begin the next stroke. A synchronized "fishtail kick"—a whiplike action using both legs together—is used. The stroke requires considerable strength and cannot be performed over great distances.

The **medley** is a 400-m individual and team event for men and women. It combines all four strokes described above. In the individual competition, the swimmer performs each stroke over a distance of 100 m. In the medley relay, each team member swims a different stroke for 100 m. The order of strokes in both competitions is as follows: backstroke, breaststroke, butterfly, and freestyle.

The program in Moscow also includes four diving events—the **platform** and **springboard** competitions for men and women. The platform is a stationary surface 10 m (32' 10") above the water. The springboard is a narrower, flexible board by which the jumping diver is propelled upward before beginning the actual dive. In both events, the diver performs acrobatic twists, turns, and somersaults before entering the water. Whether the diver comes down feet first or head first, the object is to enter the water vertically and to make as small a splash as possible. Diving is one of the few Olympic sports that is based on subjective evaluation of form and style rather than some objective or quantifiable goal.

Dives from either surface are often classified into five groups: *front; back; reverse* (front takeoff, back entry); *inward* (back takeoff, front entry); and *twisting*. Most dives in each group can be executed in three classical positions: 1) *tuck*—the body rolled into a ball, knees clasped; 2) *pike*—straight legs, bent at the hips; and 3) *layout*—the body fully extended.

RULES

Olympic swimming and diving is governed by the International Amateur Swimming Federation (FINA), founded in 1908. FINA establishes the rules and format of the competition, determines how many competitors are allowed on each team, and sets qualifying standards in each event.

Each country is allowed at least one competitor per event, regardless of the qualifying standard. The maximum number of swimmers per event from any country is three, in which case the second and third entrants must meet FINA standards. Only one team per country may compete in each relay, and the medley team must be made up of swimmers participating in other events. There are no qualifying standards in any of the relays. The total number of swimmers and divers from any nation may not exceed 33 men and 30 women.

In the swimming events, qualifying heats are held to narrow the field. The 16 fastest swimmers in the preliminary heats advance to the semifinals, from which the eight fastest move on to the finals. A similar procedure is used in diving.

The Olympic pool is 50 m (164') long and divided into eight lanes, each 2.5 m (8' 2½") wide. During competition, the water must be kept at a constant level and at a minimum temperature of +25°C (+77°F). All races except the backstroke start with the swimmers diving off the edge of the pool at the sound of a gun. In backstroke events, the swimmers start off in the water holding onto a handgrip on the wall of the pool. Always staying in the same lane, the swimmer proceeds from one end of the pool to the other, using the walls to kick off. The electronic timing device is automatically stopped when the swimmer touches the wall after his last lap.

The diving competition is more complicated but also more beautiful to watch. In the Olympics, seven judges approved by FINA evaluate each dive from different vantage points. Every diver must perform certain required dives and several optional dives from an approved list. Each dive is assigned a "degree of difficulty" (up to 3.0) based on the position in which it is executed and number of twists and turns. After each dive, the judges display their scores, which can range from 0 to 10. The highest and lowest are discarded, and the remaining scores are totaled and multiplied by the degree of difficulty. That score is divided by 5 and multiplied by 3, yielding the point total for the dive. The winner of the competition is the diver who obtains the greatest number of points.

HISTORY

Although swimming races have been held at all the modern Olympic Games, the program has undergone enormous change. In 1896 only four events were held, all freestyle races for men. Included on the program in 1900 were the 200-m backstroke, obstacle swimming, and underwater swimming. The 1904 Games saw the first breaststroke race (400 m), an event called "plunge for distance," and the first diving competition—the highboard. Springboard diving was introduced four years later. Women's swimming and diving events were not held until 1912, and even then there were only three: the 100-m freestyle, 400-m freestyle relay, and highboard diving. There were no butterfly events until the 1956 Games in Melbourne. The medley was introduced in 1960.

Even more marked than the changes in the program have been the changes in the swimming facilities. At the 1896 Games in Athens, the competitions were not held in a pool but in the cold, choppy waters of the Bay of Zea. In 1900 they were held in the river Seine near Paris. Four years later in St. Louis, an irregularly shaped "pool" was staked out in the middle of a man-made lake. The starting block was a wooden raft that bowed and even submerged in the middle under the weight of the poised swimmers. In 1908 a pool was dug out in the middle of the stadium at Shepherd's Bush in Greater London. It was not until 1964 that an indoor pool was used for Olympic swimming and diving.

CHAMPIONS

The swimming events have produced many of the greatest performances and most colorful stars in Olympic lore. Johnny Weissmuller, Buster Crabbe, and Don Schollander were among the most popular. But probably the greatest performer was Mark Spitz, who won a total of 9 gold medals, 7 in 1972. Among the women, Australia's Dawn Fraser won 4 gold and 4 silver medals in 1956, 1960, and 1964. Patricia McCormick, the U.S. diver, won the platform and springboard titles in 1952 and 1956.

TRENDS AND DEVELOPMENTS

Although swimming itself probably dates back to prehistoric man, competitive racing is still a relatively young sport. While track and field athletes seem to be approaching the limits of what is humanly possible, swimmers still have a long way to go. During the seven-day swim meet at the 1976 Games in Montreal, Olympic records were broken no less than 77 times, world records 29 times! Several important time barriers were broken: 50 seconds for the 100-m freestyle; 2 minutes for the 200-m backstroke; and 2 minutes for the women's 200-m freestyle.

Meanwhile, champion swimmers seem to be getting younger and younger. Perhaps the only sport that can boast more medal winners under the age of 16 is gymnastics. As the facilities for young swimmers are improved and made more available, as training methods become more sophisticated, and as techniques are further perfected, the Olympic medal winners will get even younger and the records will fall even faster.

1980 SUMMARY

EVENT	GOLD MEDAL WINNER	COUNTRY	TIME	OLYMPIC RECORD
Men's 100-m Freestlye:				:49.99
Men's 200-m Freestyle:				1:50.29
Men's 400-m Freestyle:				3:51.93
Men's 1,500-m Freestyle·				15:02.40
Men's 100-m Breaststroke:				1:03.11
Men's 200-m Breaststroke:				2:15.11
Men's 100-m Backstroke:				:55.49
Men's 200-m Backstroke:				1:59.19
Men's 100-m Butterfly:				:54.27
Men's 200-m Butterfly:				1:59.23
Men's 400-m Individual Medley:				4:23.68
Men's 800-m Freestyle Relay:				7:23.22
Men's 400-m Medley Relay:				3:42.22
Women's 100-m Freestyle:				:55.65
Women's 200-m Freestyle:				1:59.26
Women's 400-m Freestyle:				4:09.89
Women's 800-m Freestyle:				8:37.14
Women's 100-m Breaststroke:				1:10.86
Women's 200-m Breaststroke:				2:33.35
Women's 100-m Backstroke:				1:01.83
Women's 200-m Backstroke:				2:13.43
Women's 100-m Butterfly:				1:00.13
Women's 200-m Butterfly:				2:11.41
Women's 400-m Individual Medley:				4:42.77
Women's 400-m Freestyle Relay:				3:44.82
Women's 400-m Medley Relay:				4:07.95

EVENT	GOLD MEDAL WINNER	COUNTRY
Men's Springboard:		
Men's Platform:		
Women's Springboard:		
Women's Platform:		

TRACK AND FIELD

Dates: July 24–28, 30–August 1
Location: Central Lenin Stadium at Luzhniki, Moscow
Number of Events: 38
Held for: men, women

The running, jumping, and throwing competitions referred to collectively as *track and field,* or simply *athletics,* form the backbone of the modern Olympic Games. At the XXII Summer Games in 1980, 38 sets of medals—24 for men, 14 for women—will be awarded in track and field. This represents the greatest number of events in any Olympic sport and about one fifth of all the events on the program. Nearly 1,800 athletes from 100 nations are expected to take part, and some 1,500,000 spectators will fill Moscow's Central Lenin Stadium during the eight days of competition.

Track and field is accorded the place of honor among the Olympic sports because each competition is a simple test of some basic physical ability. Whether running, high jumping, or throwing a javelin, the track and field athlete achieves success only by making sufficient self demands. No matter how many other contestants are entered, all that counts are one's own ability and effort. Because the sport is conducted almost exclusively on an amateur basis, Olympic gold medal winners are regarded as the unofficial world champions in their particular events. The long history of Olympic track and field is rich in drama, tradition, and colorful personalities. Television viewers of the 1980 Games in Moscow will witness a new chapter in the pursuit of athletic excellence.

A full list of Olympic track and field events is given below:

RUNNING
100 meters (men, women)
200 meters (men, women)
400 meters (men, women)
800 meters (men, women)
1,500 meters (men, women)
5,000 meters (men only)
10,000 meters (men only)
Marathon (men only)
100-meter hurdles (women only)
110-meter hurdles (men only)
400-meter hurdles (men only)
3,000-meter steeplechase (men only)
4 × 100-meter relay (men, women)
4 × 400-meter relay (men, women)

WALKING
20 kilometers (men only)
50 kilometers (men only)

JUMPING
High Jump (men, women)
Long Jump (men, women)
Triple Jump (men only)
Pole Vault (men only)

THROWING (WEIGHT EVENTS)
Shot Put (men, women)
Discus (men, women)
Javelin (men, women)
Hammer (men only)

COMBINED
Decathlon (men only)
Pentathlon (women only)

HISTORY

The athletic skills displayed in a track and field meet no doubt had their origins in man's earliest activities as a hunter. Running, jumping over obstacles, and throwing stones or a spear were prerequisites of survival. But it could not have been long before such activities were engaged in for the sheer fun of competitive recreation. One needn't be an anthropologist to realize that foot races and throwing and jumping contests are age-old pastimes.

Track and field was a major sport in ancient Greece. Olympic champions were regarded as the greatest of heroes. At the first Olympic celebration in 776 B.C. a single foot race was held. The sprint was approximately 630 ft (192 m) long—or one *stade,* from which the word stadium derives. It was won by a cook named Coroebus from the city of Elis. The Games were held every four years for the next 11 centuries. Longer foot races, broad jumping, the javelin throw, the marathon, and other events were added to the program over the years. To the ancient Greeks, the Olympics were not only a sports festival but also a religious celebration and a political event. Athletes and spectators from the far reaches of the Hellenic world traveled to Olympia for the Games. Wars and trade between states were suspended. The Olympic Games remained a sacred occasion even after Greek culture and civilization began to fade. The Games finally were abolished in 393 A.D. by the Roman Emperor Theodosius I, who regarded them as pagan.

At the urgings of a small group of sports enthusiasts spurred by French Baron Pierre de Coubertin, the Olympic Games were revived in 1896. From the outset, track and field was the principle part of the program. It comprised 12 of the 43 events in the first modern Games, in which the United States began a long winning tradition by taking 9 gold, 5 silver, and 2 bronze medals. The number of events and competitors grew steadily in subsequent Olympiads. By the 1912 Games in Stockholm there were 31 events in track and field; the number of participants had grown from 59 in 1896 to 556. The year 1912 was also significant because it marked the founding of the International Amateur Athletic Federation (IAAF), the international governing body for the sport. The IAAF assumed the responsibilities of formalizing rules and regulations and of ratifying world and Olympic records. The organization continues to be the official governing body to the present day.

Another important turning point came in 1928, when women's track and field competitions were held for the first time at the Olympics. A total of 101 women vied for medals in five events—the 100-m dash, 800-m run, 4 × 100-m relay, high jump, and discus. The number of women's events increased steadily over the years, and female stars emerged. Mildred (Babe) Didrikson, considered by many to be the greatest all-around woman athlete in history, was the toast of the 1932 Games in Los Angeles. Fanny Blankers-Koen, the Dutch sprinter and hurdler, starred in 1948. In 1960, television and a U.S. sprinter named Wilma Rudolph showed the world that women's track and field was as exciting as men's competition. Rudolph won gold medals in the 100-m and 200-m dashes and the 4 × 100-m relay.

As the number of events for both men and women increased, various competitions were also dropped from the program. All told, there have been 64 different track and field events in the modern Olympic Games. The list of discontinued events includes a 60-m dash; standing high jump, standing long jump, and standing triple jump; 56-lb (25.4-kg) weight throw; ancient style discus throw; 1,500-m walk; and even a tug of war.

The record for most Olympic gold medals in track and field is held by Ray Ewry, who won 10 championships in the standing high jump, standing long jump, and standing triple jump between 1900 and 1908; Ewry's

10 gold medals are an absolute Olympic record. Paavo Nurmi, the great Finnish long distance runner, holds the record for most gold medals for a trackman in a single Olympics (5 in 1924) and most track medals overall (9 gold and 3 silver between 1920 and 1928).

RULES

The track and field events involve athletic abilities so basic that they are immediately comprehensible even to the uninitiated spectator. The rules of the actual competition are simple and straightforward. The equipment, fields and courses, and elimination procedures require some description; these are provided below in the sections on each event. What follows here is a summary of IAAF regulations concerning the number, eligibility, and comportment of participating athletes.

The full complement of track and field athletes from any nation may not exceed 126 (78 men and 48 women). In each event—except the marathon, walking races, and team relays—a country may enter one athlete regardless of entry standards set by the IAAF. However, a country may field an additional two competitors, in which case all three must meet the established standard. The Olympic qualifying standards were set by the IAAF in October 1978. Specified times, distances, or point totals must have been achieved in sanctioned competition between May 21, 1979, and July 6, 1980. The standards for each event are as follows:

EVENT	MEN	WOMEN
100 m	10.2* sec	11.3*
	10.44**	11.54**
200 m	20.8*	23.4*
	21.04**	23.64**
400 m	46.4*	52.6*
	46.54**	52.74**
800 m	1:47.4 min	2:02.8
1,500 m	3:40.0	4:10.0
5,000 m	13:35.0	
10,000 m	28:30.0	
100-m hurdles		13.4*
		13.64**
110-m hurdles	13.8*	
	14.04**	
400-m hurdles	50.4*	
	50.54**	
3,000-m steeplechase	8:30.0	
High Jump	7' 2"	6' 1½"
Long Jump	25' 7"	21' 0"
Triple Jump	53' 11½"	
Pole Vault	17' 2½"	
Shot Put	63' 8"	54' 5½"
Discus	196' 10½"	183' 9"
Javelin	265' 9"	180' 5½"
Hammer	229' 8"	
Decathlon	7,650* pts	
	7,550**	
Pentathlon		4,300* pts
		4,260**

*Hand timed   **Electrically timed

In the marathon, 20-km walking, and 50-km walking events, each country may enter a maximum of three athletes. In the relay events, each country may field only one team of four runners.

All competing athletes must wear shorts and a jersey or shirt upon which an identifying number issued by the Olympic organizing committee must be conspicuously displayed. Shoes are the most important and closely regulated item of clothing. The sole can be no more than ½ inch (13mm) thick, and the number of spikes is limited to 6 in the sole and 2 in the heel; the shoe may not be constructed so as to give the athlete any special assistance, nor may any appliance or device be used toward that end. The athlete is not required to wear shoes, however, and may opt for competing in bare feet or with shoes on one or both feet. In fact, it is quite common for high jumpers to wear a shoe only on the takeoff foot. And in 1960, Abebe Bikila of Ethiopia ran 26 mi 385 yds (42,195 m) through the streets of Rome *in bare feet* to capture the gold medal in the marathon.

Although IAAF regulations require women competitors to submit a doctor's certification as to their sex, the organization has found it necessary to require special sex-determination tests. The practice was first implemented at the 1966 European championships, and there have been several instances of ambiguous results and absenteeism. Men and women athletes are also required to take anti-doping tests. Should a competitor be found to have employed any of several specified substances which have the effect of stimulating or enhancing the strength of a performance, that athlete is disqualified from the competition.

Unsportsmanlike conduct and the assistance of a coach or teammate during the competition are both punishable by disqualification. Any physical support or conveyance of advice qualifies as assistance, and any behavior that the referee deems ungentlemanly or offensive merits said penalty. In the running events, any jostling or obstruction which impedes the progress of another competitor is also penalized by disqualification.

THE RUNNING EVENTS

Although the foot races on the Olympic program range in distance from 100 m to more than 42 km (26 mi), there are basic rules and regulations common to all. Except for the marathon, which is a road race, all are held on an oval track *(see diagram)* approximately 400 m (1,312 ft) around. The track is some 9.8 m (32 ft) wide and is divided into eight lanes, each about 1.22 m (4 ft) wide. The inside border of the track is marked by a raised curb. In each race up to and including the 400 m, runners must stay in their lanes from start to finish. In races run around the track in lanes, each runner begins at a different starting line. This *staggered start* compensates for the curves in the track and equalizes the distance in each lane. Beginning in 1968 at Mexico City, the Olympic running tracks have been made of Tartan, a synthetic resin surface, or some similar material.

In all races up to and including the 800 m, the starter uses a command equivalent to "On your marks" when the runners take their places on the starting line and "Set" when they assume a ready position. The race is begun with the firing of a gun. In races longer than 800 m, the starter merely announces "On your marks" and then fires. If a runner begins too soon—a false start—two quick shots are fired and the runners are brought back to restart the race. A competitor is disqualified for two false

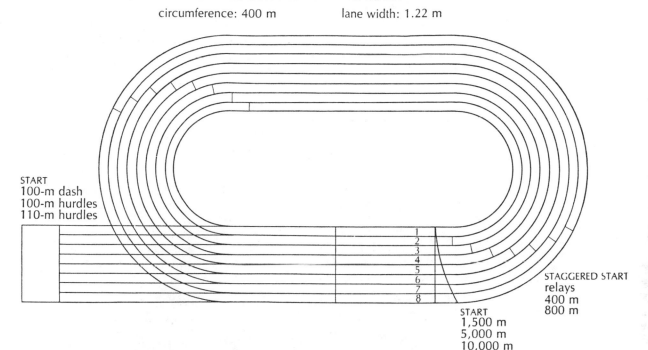

SAMPLE OLYMPIC RUNNING TRACK

circumference: 400 m   lane width: 1.22 m

START
100-m dash
100-m hurdles
110-m hurdles

1
2
3
4
5
6
7
8

STAGGERED START
relays
400 m
800 m

START
1,500 m
5,000 m
10,000 m

starts. In all races longer than one lap, the start of the final or "gun" lap is signaled by the firing of a single shot. The finish line is drawn on the ground across the width of the track. A runner completes the race when the *torso*—not the head, arms, or legs—crosses the line. At the finish line there is also a tape stretched across the track at a height of about 4 ft (1.22 m); this is only for the convenience of the runners, judges, and spectators. The race is electrically timed, and the finish is automatically photographed to determine the winner of a close race.

The two *sprints* or *dashes* on the program are the 100 m and 200 m. Pacing and jockeying for position are not necessary, as the competitors race full tilt from start to finish in their respective lanes. The runners use a crouched start, bracing their feet against starting blocks nailed into the track. Preliminary heats are held to narrow the field to eight finalists. The **100 m** is begun at the end of the long spur tangent to the oval track *(see diagram)* and is run over a straight course. The three crucial aspects of the race are the start, stride, and finish. A runner's wind is not a factor since no breaths are taken during the entire race. Maximum speed is attained by pumping the arms and kicking the knees up and straight out. A forward lean in the final stride enables the runner to cross the finish line a split second sooner. This is often the difference between victory and defeat.

Similar techniques are employed in the **200 m.** In this sprint, however, the runners begin with a staggered start and race around one curve in the track. Out of the starting blocks, the runners in the outside lanes appear to have a head start, but their relative positions become clear as they reach the final straightaway. Since the two sprint races require similar attributes—strength, concentration, and pure foot speed—they often are won by the same runner. The outstanding sprinter in the Olympic Games is universally regarded as the "world's fastest human."

The three so-called *middle distance* races are the 400 m, 800 m, and 1,500 m. The **400 m** holds a special place among track and field fans. Many consider it a long sprint—the farthest a runner can push himself at near top speed. However, the race also requires knowledge of the oppositions' abilities and sufficient experience to know when to conserve energy and when to begin the "kick," or final sprint. The race is one lap around the track; a staggered, crouched start is usually employed.

The **800 m** requires a combination of speed, stamina, and tactical judgment. It covers two full circuits of the track. The start is staggered, and the runners must keep within their lanes around the first turn. At a clearly designated spot they may cut across to the inside lane, provided they do not interfere with the other runners.

The **1,500 m,** or "metric mile," is the showcase of any track and field program. The time span (about 4 minutes) is ideal for the buildup of the spectators' excitement. The race is started on a curved line from the inside curb to the outside of the track *(see diagram)*. Unlike shorter races, the runners are not confined to lanes. In this race, perhaps more than any other, sophisticated strategies are used. The runners must know their own capabilities and be able to pace themselves accordingly.

The Olympic *long distance* races are the 5,000 m; 10,000 m; and marathon. These events are held for men only, but the International Olympic Committee (IOC) is considering the inclusion of women's long distance races in future Games. The **5,000 m** and **10,000 m** are the longest races run entirely on the track. The former is 12½ laps, the latter 25. Both are begun on the same curved starting line used in the 1,500 m. Pacing and endurance are the two most important factors of success.

The **marathon** is the most celebrated foot race in the Olympic Games. It commemorates the legendary feat of a Greek soldier said to have run from the town of Marathon to Athens to announce a military victory over the Persians. The standard distance of 26 mi 385 yds (42,195 m) was first run at the 1908 Olympics in London. It is owed to the desire of the British royal grandchildren in Windsor Castle to watch the start of the race. From there to White City Stadium in Shepherd's Bush west of London is 26 miles; the final 385 yds was run inside the stadium.

The marathon is a road race held in or near the host city of the Games. In 1980, as in the past, the last yards of the marathon will be run in the main Olympic stadium. The sight of the first runner entering the stadium and making his way around the track toward the finish line is one of the most stirring in the Olympic Games.

There are also three *hurdling* events on the track and field program—the 110 m and 400 m for men, and the 100 m for women. A hurdle *(see diagram)* is a barrier set up on the track for a runner to stride over. It consists of a horizontal wooden bar supported by two metal uprights and bases. In each race, 10 hurdles are lined up side by side in all eight lanes of the track. In the **110 m hurdles,** the barriers are 3' 6" (1.07 m) high; the first hurdle is set 13.72 m (45 ft) from the starting line, and hurdles are placed every 9.14 m (30 ft) thereafter. In the **400 m hurdles** they are 3 ft (.914 m) high; the first hurdle is 45 m (147' 8") from the starting line and then one every 35 m (114' 10"). In the women's **100 m hurdles,** the barriers are only 2' 6" (.762 m) high; the first is set up 13 m (42' 8") from the starting line, with the remaining nine hurdles at intervals of 8.5 m (27' 10").

HURDLE

Proper hurdling form is difficult to master but truly beautiful to watch. The runners seem to glide over the hurdles. Knocking over a hurdle does not automatically disqualify the runner. However, if it is knocked down *deliberately*, or if the leg or foot trails alongside the hurdle instead of directly over it, the competitor is disqualified.

A related event is the **3,000 m steeplechase.** In this 7½-lap race there is a total of 35 obstacles—28 hurdles (4 in each lap) and 7 water jumps (1 in each lap). The hurdles are 3 ft high; the water jump consists of a 3-ft hurdle in front of a pool of water 12 ft (3.66 m) long and 2' 3½" (70 cm) deep. The runner may jump cleanly over the hurdles, step on them, or vault over them with the hands; there is no penalty for stepping in the pool of water.

The only team events in the Olympic track and field competition are the two *relay* races for men and women—the **4 × 100-m relay** and **4 × 400-m relay.** A relay team consists of four runners, each of whom runs an equal distance called a leg. The runners must carry in hand a 12-inch (30-cm) cylindrical rod—called a baton—throughout the race. Each team member must be not only a strong runner but also a master of the difficult art of passing the baton. In each lane lines are drawn 10 m (32' 10") before and beyond the starting line for each leg. They mark the takeover or exchange zone. The relay to the next runner must be completed within the zone. The handoff should be made with both the passer and receiver running as close to full speed as possible. If the baton is dropped, the runner must pick it up before continuing. The fourth (and final) runner on each team is usually the fastest at the given distance; he or she is called the anchorman.

THE WALKING EVENTS

To the uninitiated spectator, the **20-km** and **50-km walking** races are no doubt the most amusing events in all Games. The stride of a race walker suggests the waddle of an arthritic duck. Although it may look funny, it is surprisingly fast and requires as much conditioning as long distance running. There are strict rules governing the technique of competitive walking. Contact with the ground may not be broken at any time. The heel of the forward foot must meet the ground before the toe of the back foot is lifted; the leg must be fully straightened for "at least one moment" with each step. The competitors are watched closely for proper heel-and-toe movement. A walker is cautioned for the first impropriety in technique, disqualified for the second.

Both walking races begin and end on the main track, but most of the distance is covered on roads outside the stadium. Refreshment and sponging stations are set up along the course.

THE JUMPING EVENTS

One of the most amazing track and field events is the **high jump.** World-class competitors often clear the crossbar at more than 1½ ft (46 cm) above their own height. It is a feat that requires spring, flawless technique, and concentration. The jump itself is made up of four parts— the approach, take-off, crossing of the bar, and landing. The approach is a fast running start down a long runway at an angle to the bar. The rules state that the jumper must take off on one foot, but they make no stipulation as to the actual style of the jump. The more traditional style is called the straddle; the jumper takes off on the foot nearest the bar, swings the other leg as high as possible, and rolls over the bar face down. At the 1968 Olympics in Mexico City, a U.S. jumper named Dick Fosbury introduced a new technique that has since replaced the straddle as the most popular. In the so-called Fosbury Flop, the jumper makes a more direct approach, pivots on the take-off foot, and crosses the bar on his back. The landing pit on the opposite side of the bar is padded with foam rubber to soften the fall.

The starting height of the bar is determined in advance by the judges and is progressively raised during the competition. Each jumper is allowed three attempts at each height; on the third miss, the contestant is eliminated. The competitors may begin jumping at the height of their choice; they may waive their turn at any height, or, after missing at one height, use their remaining attempts at a greater height. The jumper who clears the greatest height in the fewest attempts is the winner.

The **long jump,** or running broad jump, is no less amazing than its vertical counterpart. The jumper takes a long running start, accelerating almost to the speed of a sprinter. The strides are carefully measured because the jumper must take off from a flat board at the head of the landing area. Maximum distance is attained by a furious kicking motion which gives the impression of walking in air. The jumper must maintain sufficient balance to land on the heels and then fall forward. The measurement is taken from the front end of the take-off board to the nearest depression in the sand of the landing area. Each contestant takes three preliminary jumps, and the top six qualify for the final round. The finalists take three more jumps, and final standings are based on the longest of each finalist's six jumps.

One of the most outstanding athletic feats of the 20th century took place at the 1968 Olympics when Bob Beamon of the United States shattered the world long jump record by leaping an incredible 29' 2½" (8.90 m). The jump was 21½" (55 cm) longer than the previous record, an advance equal to the cumulative increases of the previous 40 years! According to most followers of track and field, Beamon's record will not be broken for many, many years.

Closely related to the long jump is the **triple jump**—sometimes called the hop, step, and jump. The contestant makes a running start and takes off from the board on one foot. He lands on the same foot (hop), takes a long stride with the other foot (step), and completes the final jump by landing on both feet. It is a difficult sequence that requires balance, coordination, and pure athletic ability. The competitor with the longest single jump is declared the winner. The competition format is the same as the one used in long jumping.

The most acrobatic jumping event is the **pole vault.** As in high jumping, the object is to clear a crossbar without knocking it down. The contestants get three attempts at each height, and the vaulter with the highest jump is the winner. The bar is considerably higher than in the high jump, however, because the contestant uses a long pole to propel himself upward. The vaulter holds the pole in his hands and races down a long runway as fast as possible. He then plants the pole in a special slot— called the vaulting box—at the end of the runway. With all his strength and the momentum of his run, he lifts himself off the ground feet first. Completely upside down as he ascends, he releases the pole and twists over the bar. It is a remarkable display of speed, strength, and body control.

Pole vaulting is one event that has undergone considerable change over the years. Although the objective has remained the same, techniques have changed noticeably and records have reached almost unbelievable heights. The main reason is the pole itself. Heavy, hard wood poles were used until about 1900, when bamboo was introduced. The world record climbed steadily during the next five decades, and it was not until the late 1950's that vaulters turned to metal poles. But the most important revolution came just a few years later when lightweight fiberglass poles were used for the first time. Because of their great flexibility, fiberglass poles provide an added spring that catapults the vaulter to even greater heights. At first an item of controversy, the fiberglass pole today is used in all world-class competition.

THE THROWING (WEIGHT) EVENTS

The four throwing events on the track and field program are the shot put, discus, javelin, and hammer. In each case, the athlete tosses a heavy object as far as possible. Each competitor makes several preliminary throws, and the leaders are then awarded three more attempts. The longest throw in the preliminary or final round wins the competition. That is the extent of the similarities between these events. The throwing styles are quite different, and the objects differ in shape and size.

The **shot put** is an iron or steel ball, 16 lbs (7.26 kg) for men and 8 lbs 13 oz (4 kg) for women. The shot is literally pushed—or put—from the shoulder with one hand. The thrower must remain inside a circle 7 ft (2.13 m) in diameter *(see diagram)*. Each throw is begun at the rear of the circle, with the shot putter's back to the landing area. The shot is held in the fingers of one hand in the hollow of the neck. The thrower hops backward across the circle, rotates 180°, and thrusts the heavy ball with full force.

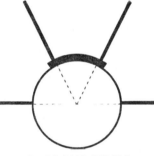

SHOT PUT CIRCLE

The classic Olympic throwing event is the **discus.** Statues of ancient Greek discus throwers attest to the long history of this event. The discus itself *(see diagram)* is a circular wooden plate with a metal rim. It is thickest at the center and gradually narrows toward the rim. A regulation men's discus is 219–221 mm (8⅝–8¹¹⁄₁₆ inches) in diameter and weighs 2 kg (4 lbs 7 oz); the women's discus is 180–182 mm (7¹⁄₁₆–7⅛ inches) in diameter and weighs 1 kg (2 lbs 3 oz). The discus is flung with one hand from a circle 2.5 m (8' 2½") in diameter. The thrower begins at the rear of the circle, with the fingers curled around the rim of the disc. Dipping the shoulder and bending the knees, the thrower takes several practice swings and begins the first pivot. Maximum leverage and thrust are attained by making several complete turns and gradually rising to full height. The discus is hurled away at the front of the circle and spins several hundred feet through the air.

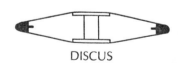

DISCUS

The **javelin** *(see diagram)* is simply a spear with a metal tip and a cord grip at the middle. A regulation men's javelin is 260–270 cm (8' 6½"– 8' 10") long and weighs 800 g (1 lb 12 oz); the women's javelin is

JAVELIN

220–230 cm (7' 2½"–7' 6½") long and weighs 600 g (1 lb 5 oz). It is held in one hand, above the shoulder. The thrower takes a running start and lets go the javelin at the throwing line. The throw is measured to the point at which the tip of the javelin hits the ground.

Although the **hammer** throw may once have been the pastime of lumberjacks and railroad workers, the implement used in modern athletic competition bears no resemblance whatsoever to any tool used for driving nails into wood or stakes into the ground. The hammer *(see diagram)* is a heavy metal ball, similar to a shot, attached to a thick wire about 4 ft (1.2 m) long with a loop grip at the end. The weight of the whole instrument is 16 lbs (7.26 kg). It is thrown from the same circle as the shot put. The thrower holds the grip with both hands, takes two or three full turns across the circle, and releases the hammer from about waist height.

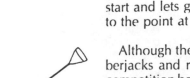

HAMMER

THE COMBINED EVENTS

Although most track and field events require unique skill and specialized training in a very narrow field of endeavor, all-around excellence remains the highest ideal of many athletes. The opportunity to display one's overall ability is provided by two very special events in the Olympic Games—the decathlon for men and the pentathlon for women. The winners of these two competitions are hailed as the world's greatest athletes.

The **decathlon** is a two-day competition consisting of 10 different events. On the first day, the athletes compete in the 100-m dash, long jump, shot put, high jump, and 400-m run, in that order. The second day's events comprise, in the following order, the 110-m hurdles, discus throw, pole vault, javelin throw, and 1,500-m run. It is not essential for a decathlete to place first in any event in order to win the gold medal. His performance is scored on the basis of a complicated point system that rewards overall ability and penalizes incompetence in any individual event. The usual formula for the scoring table, which is revised every few years by the IAAF, is to award 1,000 points for matching an established standard in a particular event. Less or more points are awarded according to the exact time, height, or distance.

The **pentathlon** is a series of five events held in one day—the 100-m hurdles, shot put, high jump, long jump, and 800-m run. A scoring system similar to that used in the decathlon is employed.

SWIFTER, HIGHER, STRONGER

A continuing controversy among track and field fans is whether there are limits to human athletic ability. How long before the final records are set? More than a few "experts" have constructed elaborate theories and complex mathematical formulas to determine not only what the limits are but when they will be reached. Sports historians compare world records from decade to decade, while physiologists try to determine maximum oxygenation efficiency or the greatest amount of stress one muscle can endure. But even the most serious researcher must admit that there are no definite answers. An athletic performance involves so many intangibles—attitude, concentration, the ability to withstand pain, to name just a few—that to speak of limits is only to speculate. One thing remains certain: as equipment, training methods, and mental conditioning techniques become more sophisticated, records will fall.

EVENT	GOLD MEDAL WINNER	COUNTRY	TIME/ DISTANCE/ POINTS	OLYMPIC RECORD
			1980 SUMMARY	
Men's 100 m:				9.9
Men's 200 m:				19.8
Men's 400 m:				43.8
Men's 800 m:				1:43.5
Men's 1,500 m:				3:34.9
Men's 5,000 m:				13:24.76
Men's 10,000 m:				27:38.4
Marathon:				2:09:55.0
Men's 110-m Hurdles:				13.24
Men's 400-m Hurdles:				47.64
Men's 3,000-m Steeplechase:				8:08.2
Men's 4 × 100-m Relay:				38.19
Men's 4 × 400-m Relay:				2:56.1
Men's 20-km Walk:				1:24:40.6
Men's 50-km Walk:				3:56:11.6
Men's High Jump:				7' 4½"
Men's Long Jump:				29' 2½"
Men's Triple Jump:				57' ¼"
Men's Pole Vault:				18' ½"
Men's Shot Put:				69' 6"
Men's Discus:				221' 5"
Men's Javelin:				310' 4'
Men's Hammer:				254' 4"
Decathlon:				8,618 pts.
Women's 100 m:				11.0
Women's 200 m:				22.37
Women's 400 m:				49.29
Women's 800 m:				1:54.94
Women's 1,500 m:				4:01.4
Women's 100-m Hurdles:				12.59
Women's 4 × 100-m Relay:				42.55
Women's 4 × 400-m Relay:				3:19.23
Women's High Jump:				6' 4"
Women's Long Jump:				22' 4½"
Women's Shot Put:				69' 5"
Women's Discus:				226' 4"
Women's Javelin:				216' 4"
Pentathlon:				4,801 pts.

VOLLEYBALL

Dates: men—July 20–30, August 1–2
women—July 21–26, 28–29, 31–August 1
Location: The Small Sports Arena at Luzhniki, Moscow
Number of Events: 2 tournaments
Held for: men, women

Volleyball, like basketball, is one of the few "invented" sports that gained sufficient international popularity to be included on the Olympic program. The game originally was intended for middle-aged businessmen who found basketball too strenuous. When played seriously, however, the game requires speed, agility, and teamwork. A volleyball smashed over the net was once timed at more than 110 miles (177 km) per hour.

HISTORY

Volleyball was invented in 1895 by William G. Morgan, director of the Y.M.C.A. in Holyoke, Mass. He took the bladder out of a soccer ball, strung a tennis net across the gym, and devised rules for the game he called "mintonette." Although the sport did not catch on so quickly as basketball, it gradually spread across the United States. The worldwide growth of the sport culminated in 1964 at the Tokyo Olympics when tournaments for men and women were held. As in the case of many other sports, the exposure provided by the Olympics brought even greater interest. The number of international tournaments, the size and enthusiasm of audiences, and the quality of play have been increasing ever since.

A look at the medalists in the four men's and women's Olympic tournaments (below) reveals the domination of Soviet and Japanese teams. Poland, Czechoslovakia, and the two Koreas also have been strong.

PAST MEDAL WINNERS

		GOLD	SILVER	BRONZE
1964	men	URS	TCH	JPN
	women	JPN	URS	POL
1968	men	URS	JPN	TCH
	women	URS	JPN	POL
1972	men	JPN	GDR	URS
	women	URS	JPN	PRK
1976	men	POL	URS	CUB
	women	JPN	URS	KOR

RULES

Volleyball is played with six players on a side. The three stationed near the net are called the "right forward," "center forward," and "left forward." The three lined up to the rear are designated the "backs." The net is 2.43 m (8 ft) high in men's competition and 2.24 m (7' 4¼") in women's competition. The right back begins play by serving the ball into the opponents' court. The ball must go over the net without hitting the floor and be returned by the opposing team. Play continues until a team fails to return the ball. No more than three touches of the ball are allowed on each side. Points are scored only by the serving team. If the opponents win the volley, they win the right to serve for the next point. At each change of service the players on the serving team rotate clockwise. The game ends when a team reaches 15 points and leads by at least 2. Three out of five games wins the match.

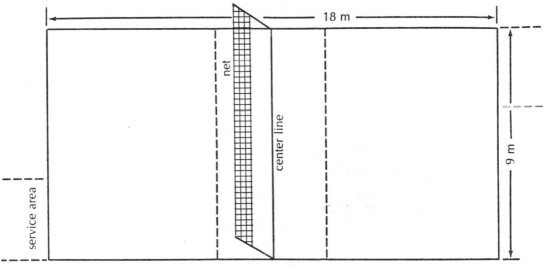

OLYMPIC VOLLEYBALL COURT

FORMAT

The volleyball tournament at the 1980 Moscow Olympics is limited to 10 men's teams and 8 women's teams. There is a maximum of 12 players per team. In the men's tournament, the teams are divided into two groups of five. Then they play a round-robin schedule within each group. The team with the best record in each group then plays the second best team in the other group. The winners of these matches play each other for the gold and silver medals; the losers play for the bronze medal. In women's competition, the teams are divided into two groups of four, and final rankings are determined in the same manner.

REGULATION BALL
circumference: 65–67 cm
weight: 250–260 g

1980 SUMMARY

FINAL STANDINGS
(men's)

GOLD:

SILVER:

BRONZE:

FINAL STANDINGS
(women's)

GOLD:

SILVER:

BRONZE:

WATER POLO

Dates: July 23-25, 27-29, 31—August 1
Location: Swimming Pool of Central Lenin Stadium, Moscow
Olympiisky Sports Center, Moscow
Number of Events: 1 tournament
Held for: men only

Water polo is a team sport that has much in common with hockey, handball, soccer, and other games in which the object is to propel a ball into a goal. It is unique, however, in that it is played in water and requires the stamina to swim continuously for an entire match. Because most of the offensive and defensive maneuvering takes place underwater, many spectators do not realize that it is also one of the roughest sports on the Olympic program.

Twelve teams are competing in the 1980 Olympic water polo tournament. A maximum of 11 players, including reserves, is allowed on each team. The tournament is for men only.

RULES AND REGULATIONS

In Olympic competition, the field of play *(see diagram)* must be 20 m (65' 7") wide and 30 m (98' 5") from goal line to goal line. The water must nowhere be less than 1.8 m (5' 11") deep. The goals at each end are 3 m (9' 10") wide, with the top crossbar 90 cm (2' 11") above the surface of the water. Markings on both sides of the pool denote the goal lines, lines 2 and 4 m (6' 7" and 13' 1") from each goal line, and a center line.

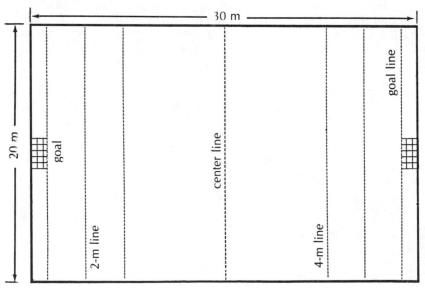

OLYMPIC WATER POLO FIELD

Each team consists of seven players, including one goalkeeper, and four substitutes. All players must wear a special cap with a number on each side. One team wears dark blue caps and the other team white caps, except for the goalkeepers, who wear red caps. Each goalkeeper wears cap No. 1 and his teammates Nos. 2 through 11. The match is supervised by two referees, two goal judges, and a timekeeper.

The duration of the match is four periods of 5 minutes each, with a 2-minute interval between periods. The teams change ends before each new period. At the beginning of each period the teams line up on their respective goal lines, and the referee blows a whistle to start play. The ball is released from a cage at the bottom of the pool and rises to the center of the playing area. The player who first reaches the ball takes possession for his team. By pushing the ball along the water and passing it from player to player, each team attempts to advance toward the opposing goal. A goal is scored by passing the ball *fully* over the goal line with any part of the body except a clenched fist. The goal judge indicates that a point has been scored by holding up a red and white flag. The goalkeeper, whose job it is to prevent the ball from entering the goal, has special privileges not accorded the other players—within the 4-meter area he may stand and walk on the bottom of the pool, punch the ball with his fist, jump from the bottom of the pool, and touch the ball with both hands.

For an ordinary foul—such as standing on the floor of the pool or holding the ball underwater—the penalty is a free throw from the point of the infraction; if the foul is committed within the 2-meter line, the free throw is taken from the line itself. In the case of a major foul—such as holding, sinking, or kicking the opponent—the offending player is ordered out of the water for one minute or until a goal is scored, whichever is shorter; also, the opposing team is awarded a free throw. The most severe punishment is a penalty throw, a direct shot at the goal. A penalty throw is awarded if one of several fouls, including "acts of brutality," is committed against an attacking player within the 4-meter zone.

FORMAT

The 12 teams that take part in the Olympic tournament are determined on the basis of elimination matches held prior to the Games. The qualifiers are divided into three groups (A, B, and C) of four teams each. Each team plays every other team in its group, and the best two of each proceed to Group D. The teams in Group D all play each other to determine the final standings from 1 to 6. The third and fourth place teams in each initial group advance to Group E and play each other for the last six places in the standings.

The ranking of teams in each group is based on a point system—2 points for each match won, 1 point for a draw, and 0 points for a loss. If two teams end up with an equal number of points, precedence is given to the team with the largest differential between goals scored and goals allowed.

1980 SUMMARY

FINAL STANDINGS

GOLD:

SILVER:

BRONZE:

WEIGHTLIFTING

Dates: July 20–24, 26–30
Location: Izmailovo Palace of Sports, Moscow
Number of Events: 10 weight classes
Held for: men only

He expands his immense chest to the maximum, and pulls tight the wide waist belt which he wears to prevent a hernia. Rubbing chalk dust in his hands for a secure grip, he walks slowly across the stage and stands above the barbell. Staring into space, he tries to imagine himself lifting the great weight. Finally, he crouches down and grasps the iron bar. In a burst of strength he brings the 500 pounds first to his shoulders and then, wavering ever so slightly, high above his head.

Weightlifting is perhaps the most stirring display of pure strength and mental discipline in the Olympic Games. Television viewers of the 1980 competition are unlikely soon to forget the feats of these, the world's strongest men. Weightlifting is enormously popular in the Soviet Union and plans for the Moscow competition have been given special attention by Olympic organizers. The Izmailovo Palace of Sports has a seating capacity of 5,000 and a separate arena in which the athletes can warm up. Competitions will be held in 10 weight classes, one more than at the 1976 Games. A new 100-kg (220 lb-7 oz) division was added to the program by the International Weightlifting Federation (IWF). The full list of weight classes is given below:

	not	
Flyweight	exceeding	52 kg (114 lbs 10 oz)
Bantamweight	"	56 kg (123 lbs 7 oz)
Featherweight	"	60 kg (132 lbs 4 oz)
Lightweight	"	67.5 kg (148 lbs 13 oz)
Middleweight	"	75 kg (165 lbs 6 oz)
Light Heavyweight	"	82.5 kg (181 lbs 14 oz)
Middle Heavyweight	"	90 kg (198 lbs 7 oz)
First Heavyweight	"	100 kg (220 lbs 7 oz)
Second Heavyweight	"	110 kg (242 lbs 8 oz)
Super Heavyweight	over	110 kg

RULES

In international amateur weightlifting, all lifts must be performed on a square platform measuring 4 m × 4 m (13 ft × 13 ft). If a contestant staggers off the platform under the weight of the barbells, the lift is declared illegal. Every lift is evaluated by three referees who sit immediately in front of the platform. Each referee must judge whether a lift is executed according to the IWF rules of style. His decision is displayed by means of a light. A white light indicates that the referee has approved the lift; a red light indicates that he has not. The lift is deemed legal if it is approved by at least two of the three referees.

Contestants in each weight class must lift the barbell in two different styles—the "two-hand clean and jerk" and the "two-hand snatch" (described below). Each lifter begins at whatever weight level he chooses and is permitted three attempts in each style. The second attempt must be at least 5 kg (11 lbs) heavier than the first, and the third attempt at least 2.5 kg (5½ lbs) heavier than the second. If a contestant does not successfully execute a lift, he may try again at the same weight or else have it increased; under no circumstance may the weight of the barbell be reduced. The weights of the heaviest lift in each style are added together, and the lifter with the highest total wins the competition. In the case of a tie, the competitor with the lower body weight is the winner.

STYLES OF LIFTING

In both styles of Olympic weightlifting, the lifter grasps the barbell with both hands, palms down. In the **two-hand clean and jerk** (*see diagram below*), the barbell must be brought up to the shoulders in one clean movement. The lifter may then move his legs and adjust his weight in any way he chooses. However, before beginning the jerk phase of the lift, he must come to an upright position with his feet on an even line. Using all the strength he can muster from his legs and chest, he must then bring the barbell to full arms' extension above the head.

TWO-HAND CLEAN AND JERK

In the **two-hand snatch** (*see diagram below*), the barbell must be lifted from the floor to the arms-extended position in a single, continuous movement. The weight must be held aloft until both feet are brought in line and the head referee signals to lower it. The snatch requires considerably more strength than the clean and jerk, and less weight is lifted.

TWO-HAND SNATCH

HISTORY

The sport of weightlifting has undergone considerable change since the first Olympic competition in 1896. Two events were held that year—the one- and two-hand dumbbell contests. The dumbbell was a simple iron rod with solid balls attached at each end. The champions of 1896, Launceston Elliot of Great Britain and Viggo Jensen of Denmark, more resembled circus strongmen than the Olympic weightlifters of today. No weightlifting events were held in 1900, but the one- and two-hand dumbbell contests were on the program again in 1904 and 1906. There was no further competition until the 1920 Games in Antwerp. The dumbbell events were replaced by the snatch, clean and jerk, and press styles of lifting. Disc barbells were used for the first time, and weight classes were introduced to give smaller athletes a chance to win medals. Over the years, the number of weight divisions increased steadily from the five established in 1920. The styles of lifting remained unchanged until 1972, when the press was omitted from the competition.

Since it first took part in the Olympics in 1952, the Soviet Union has fielded by far the most successful weightlifting teams. Lifters from Bulgaria, Poland, and the other Eastern European countries have been the most serious challengers to Soviet supremacy. Of the 18 gold medals awarded in weightlifting at the 1972 and 1976 Olympics, 10 went to the USSR, 5 to Bulgaria, and 1 each to Hungary, Norway, and Poland.

TRENDS AND DEVELOPMENTS

Comparing the performances of Olympic weightlifters over the past 50 years provides dramatic evidence of the awesome feats of present-day iron men. For example, the gold medalist in the heavyweight division at the 1928 Games lifted a combined weight of 250 kg (550 lbs) in the snatch and clean and jerk; in 1976, the winner in the *bantamweight* division surpassed that amount by some 13 kg (28.6 lbs).

Part of the reason for this rapid development has been the realization that confidence, concentration, and a positive mental approach are as important as pure strength. Mind over body is the guiding principle. How much a man can lift is left literally to the imagination.

1980 SUMMARY

WEIGHT CLASS	GOLD MEDAL WINNER	COUNTRY	WEIGHT
Flyweight:			
Bantamweight:			
Featherweight:			
Lightweight:			
Middleweight:			
Light Heavyweight:			
Middle Heavyweight:			
First Heavyweight:			
Second Heavyweight:			
Super Heavyweight:			

WRESTLING

Dates: Greco-Roman—July 20–24
Freestyle—July 27–31
Location: Central Army Sports Club, Moscow
Number of Events: Greco-Roman—10 weight classes
Freestyle—10 weight classes
Held for: men only

Wrestling is probably the oldest and most basic form of recreational combat. Its origins are no doubt prehistoric. The first rules were written in Athens around 900 B.C., and the sport was introduced into the ancient Olympic Games in 708 B.C. There have been surprisingly few changes since that time. Wrestling is a highly instinctive sport that requires alertness, resiliency, and above all, strength.

Amateur wrestling is divided into two categories—Greco-Roman and freestyle. In Greco-Roman wrestling it is against the rules to grasp the opponent below the hips, trip him, or actively use the legs to execute a hold. These tactics are not forbidden in freestyle wrestling. At the 1980 Olympic Games in Moscow, there are elimination tournaments in 10 weight classes for both Greco-Roman and freestyle wrestling.

WEIGHT CLASSES

The 10 weight classes used in Olympic wrestling competition are established by the International Amateur Wrestling Federation (FILA). The names and weight limitations for each class are given below:

	not exceeding	
Paperweight	not exceeding	48 kg (105 lbs 13 oz)
Flyweight	"	52 kg (114 lbs 10 oz)
Bantamweight	"	57 kg (125 lbs 10 oz)
Featherweight	"	62 kg (136 lbs 11 oz)
Lightweight	"	68 kg (149 lbs 15 oz)
Welterweight	"	74 kg (163 lbs 2 oz)
Middleweight	"	82 kg (180 lbs 12 oz)
Light Heavyweight	"	90 kg (198 lbs 7 oz)
Heavyweight	"	100 kg (220 lbs 7 oz)
Super Heavyweight	over	100 kg

Only one wrestler per country may be entered in each weight class of Greco-Roman and freestyle competition; no reserves are allowed.

RULES AND SCORING

The mat used in both Greco-Roman and freestyle wrestling (*see diagram*) must be at least 10 cm (4 inches) thick and made of plastic or foam rubber. The center wrestling area is 9–10 m (29'6"–32'10") in diameter. It is surrounded by a red band 1 m (3' 3") wide, called the passivity zone. Another circle, 1 m in diameter, is traced in the very middle of the center area. To avoid accidents, the wrestling surface is bordered by a protection area 1.2–1.5 m (3'11"–4'11") wide.

All holds are started at the innermost circle. They end when both feet of one wrestler and one foot of the other enter the passivity zone. At this

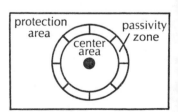

OLYMPIC WRESTLING MAT

time the referee shouts "Zone!" and the wrestlers return to the center to begin again. Each bout consists of three 3-minute periods—a total of 9 minutes actual wrestling time. There is a 1-minute interval between periods, during which a coach and a masseur may meet with each athlete. If the referee declares a fall or disqualification, the bout ends before the scheduled time. A fall occurs when a wrestler's shoulders are pinned to the mat for one second. Disqualification is the penalty for excessive stalling, breach of discipline, persistent use of illegal holds, and other violations.

During the course of a bout, the referee awards 1 to 4 points for the successful execution of specified moves and holds. Barring a fall or disqualification, the wrestler with the most points at the end of the bout is declared the winner. Points are awarded for takedowns (bringing the opponent to the mat from a standing position) controlling the opponent while on the mat, putting the opponent in a "dangerous position" (in which the angle of his back relative to the mat is 90° or less); escapes; reversals; combinations· near pins· and other actions. Bonus points are earned for lifting the opponent completely off the ground, dominant control throughout the match, and other extraordinary accomplishments. The referee signals the number of points awarded by holding up the appropriate number of fingers. The spectator is kept abreast of the point totals by an electronic scoreboard.

In both styles of wrestling, hair pulling, scratching, grabbing the throat, twisting the fingers or toes, driving an elbow or knee into the opponent's back or abdomen, scissor holds, and similar tactics are strictly forbidden.

FORMAT

The elimination procedure in each weight class is not entirely based on whether the wrestlers win or lose a particular match. Rather, contestants are not eliminated until they have accumulated a total of 6 penalty marks. After every bout, up to 4 penalty marks are assigned to either or both of the wrestlers depending on how the bout was decided. A wrestler who loses by fall or disqualification receives 4 penalty marks; the winner receives none. A wrestler who loses a bout in which 10 or more points are scored receives 3.5 penalty marks; the winner is assigned 0.5. When less than 10 points are scored, the loser receives 3 penalty marks, the winner 1. In the case of a draw, both wrestlers are assigned 2 penalty marks.

Preliminary rounds continue until only three wrestlers are left. In the finals, these three contestants wrestle each other on a round-robin basis. However, if any of the finalists has fought any of the others in a preliminary round, their bout in the final round is not held. First, second, and third place in the final round are determined by the number of penalty marks that each of the three wrestlers has received in his bouts with the other two.

TRENDS

In recent years, the FILA has enhanced the quality of amateur wrestling by instituting and enforcing rules against running off the mat, avoiding contact, not attacking forcefully, and other passive tactics. This approach is articulated in Section C, Article 3 of the FILA rulebook, under the heading "Total Wrestling Concept":

" 'Total Wrestling' is a concept demanding full aggressive activity by the wrestlers. Wrestlers must be mentally and physically prepared to combat in the center of the mat throughout the entire match and be willing to take risks in order to win.

"Defensive wrestling must be aggressive counter-wrestling, not merely moves avoiding combative situations. All such defensive passivity and non-action will be vigorously discouraged by officials. Rules and penalties will be forcefully applied to obtain spectacular and aggressive wrestling—Total Wrestling—in all Olympic and World Wrestling Competition."

1980 SUMMARY

Greco-Roman

WEIGHT CLASS	GOLD MEDAL WINNER	COUNTRY
Paperweight:		
Flyweight:		
Bantamweight:		
Featherweight:		
Lightweight:		
Welterweight:		
Middleweight:		
Light Heavyweight:		
Heavyweight:		
Super Heavyweight:		

Freestyle

WEIGHT CLASS	GOLD MEDAL WINNER	COUNTRY
Paperweight:		
Flyweight:		
Bantamweight:		
Featherweight:		
Lightweight:		
Welterweight:		
Middleweight:		
Light Heavyweight:		
Heavyweight:		
Super Heavyweight:		

YACHTING

Dates: July 21–24, 27–29
Location: Gulf of Tallinn, USSR
Number of Events: 6
Held for: men and women

Yachting is one of the least known sports on the Olympic program. Many are not even aware that it is included, and others are misled by its name. Yachting in the Olympics is the racing of sailing craft considerably smaller than most modern pleasure boats.

HISTORY

Yachts (from the Dutch *jachtschiff*—hunting boat) were first developed in Holland during the 16th century as fast-sailing hunting vessels and pursuit ships against pirates. Gradually, the yachts were built smaller, faster, and without armaments. They were favored by Dutch noblemen and British royalty. The first yacht club was founded in 1820 at Cork, Ireland.

Plans for an exhibition regatta near Athens were made for the first modern Olympics in 1896. However, the event had to be canceled because of a storm. The first Olympic sailing events were held in 1900, with Great Britain winning the Open class. Competitions were also held in the .5 ton (454 kg), .5–1 ton (454–907 kg), 1–2 ton (907–1,814 kg), 2–3 ton (1,814–2,721 kg), 3–10 ton (2,721–9,072 kg), 10–20 ton (9,072–18,143 kg) classes. In these, Britain and France took two golds; Germany and the United States one each. There was no yachting at the 1904 and 1906 Games, but competitions were held in the 6-, 7-, 8-, and 12-meter classes in 1908. For the first and only time in the Olympics, motorboating was included in the 1908 program. France won the title.

Norway has won the most gold medals in Olympic yachting, but all the Scandinavian countries have generally done well. The United States, which won the Star and 8-meter classes in home waters in 1932, and Great Britain have also been particularly strong over the years. Paul B. Elvström of Denmark became the first Olympian to win individual gold medals in four successive Games when he won the Finn Monotype Class in 1948, 1952, 1956, and 1960. Six golds for yachting were awarded in both 1972 and 1976. At these Games, Australian, British, and West German yachts were the big winners—capturing two golds each.

CLASSES

The International Yacht Racing Union (IYRU), the governing body of Olympic competition, is staging races in six international classes at the 1980 Games. The dimensions of the yachts for each class follow:

Finn—length 4.50 m
width 1.51 m
sail area 10 m^2
weight 145 kg

470—length 4.70 m
width 1.68 m
sail area 13.5 m^2
weight 118 kg

Tornado—length 6.10 m
width 3.05 m
sail area 21.8 m²
weight 148 kg

Star—length 6.92 m
width 1.73 m
sail area 26.5 m²
draft 0.925 m
weight 662 kg

Soling—length 8.15 m
width 1.90 m
sail area 21.7 m²
draft 1.30 m
weight 1,035 kg

Flying Dutchman—length 6.05 m
width 1.70 m
sail area 14.37 m²
weight 160 kg

**SAMPLE
YACHTING COURSE**

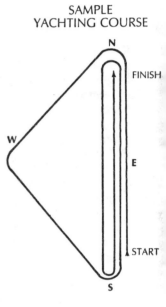

FORMAT

Seven races are held for each class, six of which are used in the final scoring. Points are awarded on the basis of finishing position in each race. Final rankings are determined by the fewest total points.

Each participating country is allowed one yacht in each class. The number of yachtsmen from each country may not exceed 16, including four reserves. More than 250 yachts from approximately 50 nations are being entered in 1980. The Finn and 470 classes are the most popular.

COURSES

Three courses have been laid out for the Olympic competition in 1980, all in the Baltic Sea near Tallinn, Estonia. One course, for the Finn and 470 classes, is laid off the Pirita estuary less than one mile from the new yacht club at Tallinn. Another course, for the Star and Tornado classes, cuts across the middle of the Gulf of Tallinn. The third course, for the Soling and Flying Dutchman classes, exposes the boats to strong northwestern and southwestern winds.

1980 SUMMARY

CLASS	GOLD MEDAL WINNER	COUNTRY
Finn:		
470:		
Tornado:		
Star:		
Soling:		
Flying Dutchman:		

FINAL MEDAL STANDINGS
1980 SUMMER GAMES

COUNTRY	ABBREVIATION	GOLD	SILVER	BRONZE	TOTAL
Argentina	ARG				
Australia	AUS				
Austria	AUT				
Belgium	BEL				
Brazil	BRA				
Bulgaria	BUL				
Canada	CAN				
Cuba	CUB				
Czechoslovakia	TCH				
Denmark	DEN				
Egypt	EGY				
Ethiopia	ETH				
Finland	FIN				
France	FRA				
German Dem. Rep.	GDR				
Germany	GER				
Ghana	GHA				
Great Britain	GBR				
Greece	GRE				
Hungary	HUN				
India	IND				
Iran	IRN				
Ireland	IRL				
Israel	ISR				
Italy	ITA				
Jamaica	JAM				
Japan	JPN				
Kenya	KEN				
Mexico	MEX				
Netherlands	HOL				
New Zealand	NZL				
North Korea	PRK				
Norway	NOR				
Pakistan	PAK				
Poland	POL				
Portugal	POR				
Rumania	ROM				
South Korea	KOR				
Spain	ESP				
Sweden	SWE				
Switzerland	SUI				
Thailand	THA				
Turkey	TUR				
USSR	URS				
United States	USA				
Yugoslavia	YUG				
_____	___				
_____	___				
_____	___				
_____	___